The
Tempest
Society

Bouchra
Khalili

The Tempest Society

Bouchra Khalili

Book Works

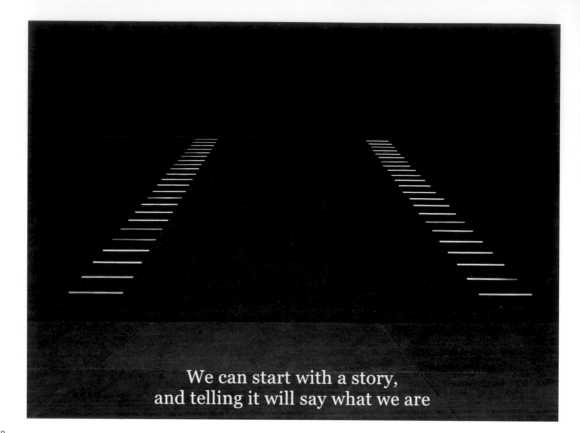

We can start with a story,
and telling it will say what we are

They stream through streets, occupied factories, cinemas, village squares, theatres

They bear a single name, one single name for them all

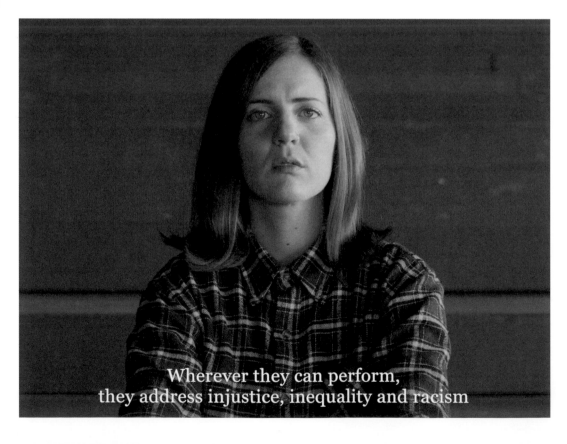

Wherever they can perform,
they address injustice, inequality and racism

✳ ΣΥΝΑΓΜΑ 20,

✳ Π

✳ ΗΛΙΑΣ

✳ ΑΛ

✳ ΤΑ ΠΑΙΔΙΑ

ΟΙ 300
✳

✳ΜΑ

AZMENT

* ΓΑΝΙ
*

* ΚΑΤΕΡΙΝΑ
*

ΑΞΕΙΦΑ

Κ

* ΣΥΝΤΑΓΜΑ
2015

Staged in Solidarity Bouchra Khalili's *The Tempest Society*

In the first and final scenes of Bouchra Khalili's film *The Tempest Society* (2017), we see the empty stage of the Athens Festival theatre on 260 Peiraios Street, a vast and desolate space that has seen countless performances yet now bears witness to the distant whisper of Athens. Through its stained windows, we see the trees rocking in the wind, while inside the harsh neon lights illuminate the floors of the post-industrial building, one of many in that part of the city.

Three main characters – Isavella, Elias and Giannis – populate the stage in *The Tempest Society*, embodying a multitude of voices – most strongly their own. Looking directly into or just past the camera, they blend their own first hand experiences of racism and xenophobia with quotations from the Albanian writer and journalist Gazmend Kapllani, who moved to Greece in 1991 and documented some of those experiences in his book *My Name is Europe* (2010). Isavella, Elias and Giannis, with whom Khalili worked to develop the script of the film, are not professional actors. Constantly switching between historical citation and personal narrative, they personify a recurrent motif in Khalili's practice: Pier Paolo Pasolini's 'civic poet', speaking through the individual to mobilise the collective, societal voice.

One of the principal historical citations in the film is Al Assifa ('The Tempest' in Arabic), a political theatre group founded by Mohamed Bachiri (Mokhtar), Geneviève Clancy and Philippe Tancelin active in Paris between 1972 and 1978. The interventions, street plays, theatre performances, demonstrations and political gatherings performed by Mokhtar, Clancy and Tancelin, as well as temporary members of the collective, made little distinction between theatre and life, ensuring action in both realms to fight racism by demanding humane working and living conditions for migrant workers, and advocating equality and solidarity. In the first act of the film, Isavella, Elias and Giannis are joined on stage by Philippe Tancelin, the only living member of the original group. He is reading – in French, in the first person plural – from the Al Assifa manifesto *Les Tiers Idées* (1977), while the others – in Greek, in the third person plural – speak about the ways in which Al Assifa addressed the pressing political and social conditions of its time, covering their faces with photographs of Mokhtar, Clancy and Tancelin and later adding photographs of Pasolini and documentation of Al Assifa performances.

It is a key moment in *The Tempest Society*, which allows the stage to become a silent protagonist in the work. The historical figure of Philippe is discussed and at the same time present as a body, as a voice. The faces of Isavella, Elias and Giannis are hidden behind the masks of the Al Assifa members as well as scenes of their political theatre that serve as historical counterparts to the theatre the non-actors are enacting in that very moment. After Philippe walks off the stage, the physical masks are taken off, yet their residue remains. The stage, an empty theatre at the beginning and soon to be vacant again at the end of the film, is exhibited as an interlocutory device, connecting dots in a history of solidarity between Al Assifa and the manifestations of resistance in Athens today.

From that moment on, Khalili multiplies the characters in the film, marking Paris 1972–1978 and Athens 2016 as two temporal and spatial co-ordinates between and after which the European Dream – a vision of Europe as an open, tolerant, and democratic society – is fully destabilised. Isavella, Elias and Giannis are joined by other protagonists, sometimes as actual bodies on stage, in other instances as images, sounds, words or historical incarnations: Philippe, Geneviève and Mokhtar as Al Assifa; Pasolini who wrote that 'there is no poetry other than real action'; Alexandros Panagoulis, who played a key role in overthrowing the Regime of the Colonels in Greece; one of the leaders of the migrant workers' hunger strike in Thessaloniki and Athens in January 2011; Abdu, Rozina and Abas, who are announced by Elias as characters from Kapllani's novel; the 12,000 refugees in Aleppo in 1922; the thousands of refugees coming to Greece from Syria, Iraq and Afghanistan in 2015; Malek, who, tired of being reduced to the stigma of 'refugee', started a theatre group with the children and young adults around him; the five young Syrian refugees who were arrested by the police in 2016 for using toy guns in a theatre play; the people voting όχι ('No!') at the Greek bailout referendum in 2015; and the 25,000 or 50,000 or more protestors at Syntagma Square in Athens following the referendum.

Together, these 'characters' form a multitudinous assembly or, as Khalili calls it, a constellation of people across different places and different times. Seeing them come together on the imaginary (and actual) stage that Khalili produces through images, words, bodies, and voices allows for a more profound understanding of the injustices that demand solidarity, and prompts us to ask which battles unite us.

It is here that the stage itself returns as a pivotal character in the film. In the scene entitled 'Assembly', the three non-actors identified as Isavella, Elias and Giannis watch a film on stage showing the occupation of Syntagma square in Athens in 2011. We see, in alternating takes, their silhouettes from behind and the flickering light of the projector on their faces. Here and throughout The Tempest Society, the protagonists observe other characters while being watched by us. In these moments – simultaneous manifestations of actor, spectator, witness, agent and commentator – the stage, as a self-reflexive mechanism, conditions all actions and words uttered by the personages in the film to be as much a version of themselves as an incarnation of others, thereby solidifying solidarity as the governing principle of Khalili's film.

Though the theatre is foundational to the project, The Tempest Society is never performed live: it manifests as a film. Khalili's approach to cinematography is often imbued with elements of theatricality and liveliness or life, though rarely as apparent as in this film. The stage may be a continuous presence, the language may be reminiscent of a theatre script (in part developed with the non-actors), and references to the politics of the theatre recur throughout the film, yet the technique and rhythm of the work is unequivocally connected to film montage. The chapters, all titled, mark the transitions between scenes in the film and the editing follows that pace, rather than the pace of a curtain opening, actors coming in or props being moved. Moreover, there is rarely a totality to the stage – that all-encompassing frame of the theatre – since we only see the characters as the camera has filmed them, from a distance or at closer range, from the back or front, etc. (There is one notable exception to this, namely the animated part of the film that provides a speculative account of the aforementioned arrest of the Syrian refugees using toy guns for their theatre play. In this part the curtain draws at the beginning and closes at the end, and the whole scene takes place in the space of the theatre frame.) The lens of the camera is the only audience here and Khalili uses it to activate the theatre's performative properties in a cinematic *dispositif*. However, rather than presenting the film in a black box, as one might expect, the artist insists on *The Tempest Society* being shown as a video installation in a visual arts context, i.e. the exhibition space, continuously complicating the codes and boundaries of various artistic disciplines and spaces.

As a video installation, *The Tempest Society* premiered in documenta in 2017, the fourteenth installment of the quinquennial exhibition that took place, for the first time, in Athens *and* its historical birthplace Kassel. Challenging the political, cultural and economic conditions of documenta in relation to its own institutional history, artistic director Adam Szymczyk and his curatorial team (which, for the sake of full disclosure, I was part of) conceived documenta 14 as a bifurcated platform across the two cities in response to the parameters of our time: from the economic violence inflicted by neoliberalism, and the financial criminalisation of the Southern European states by the European Union, to the politics of debt and restitution governing global North and South relations, the histories of colonialism, and techniques of neo-imperialism, displacement and dispossession, and so forth. In brief, we proposed the poles of Athens and Kassel be a prism through which to *act* as artists, cultural producers, publics, politicians and policy makers, scholars and writers within the present political and cultural circumstances.

In his essay for the documenta 14 Reader, Szymczyk placed the exhibition in parallel to Antonin Artaud's concept of 'the theatre and its double', invoking the author's separation between the theatre on the one hand and reality (or life) on the other. In Szymczyk's reading, 'the theatre and its double' is both a literal reference – that is to say, Kassel the stage of representation as the perpetual home of documenta, and Athens the place where life occurs – and an enactment of Artaud's artistic mission that the stage of representation can no longer be a safe space or a haven of detachment.

The Tempest Society, embedded in this exhibition and enacting it on multiple levels, fully implicates all who step on the stage, including us. The stage is performed as a character, its mechanisms laid bare. Khalili's stage is not one of representation, nor does she project the image of history; it is neither theatre nor its double. Rather, Isavella, Elias, Giannis, Malek, Philippe and all the others, as non-actors, embody the political and social conditions that made them who they are, connected to the ones who came before and who will follow. The uninhabited stage that manifests as a visual echo at the beginning and the end of the film appears to be a border, an architectural demarcation of the space between outside and inside, on stage and off stage. More accurately, it is a reminder that the *polis,* the city that is barely visible through the windows of the Athens Festival theatre, and its *demos,* the people who inhabit it, have moved inside, populating Khalili's theatre of democracy, *The Tempest Society*.

16

Geneviève
passed away in 2005

Mokhtar,
in 2010

Only
Philippe remains

20

They left
only a few photos

Some film footage

And a book,
written on the eve of their separation,

Platform for Al Assifa, 1973
from *Les Tiers Idées*, Geneviève Clancy and Philippe Tancelin

ARTICLE I

Are we a theatre company in the traditional sense
of the term? No, we are a group that, having led
and still leading the fight for the acceptance of
migrant workers' rights, took hold of the weapon
of theatre to efficiently carry on with its
struggle. We are born from reality, in the fight.

ARTICLE II

Assifa is a collective made up of migrant workers
and French workers; directly taking part in the
movements and the struggles of the migrant workers
in France; our work is collective and the work of
each person belongs to all, based on the respect
of those principles.

ARTICLE III

Our objectives: to present the life and struggle
of migrant workers in France; to work on the
setting up of a cultural front in immigration in
order to create a real unity between migrant workers
and French workers. We want to spread, develop
and promote the cultural expression of migrant
workers in France in all fields. Against the
situation of being non-cultured that is imposed
on migrant workers, against cultural racism, we
work at promoting the cultures of origin in the
respect of differences. Our aim is to make every
cultural event accessible to all.

ARTICLE IV

In order to do that we use theatre, cinema, dance
and all street events where the identity of each
person from each community of workers can be
expressed. The working class is without borders,
we perform in Arabic and French, according to the
audience, and depending on the shows.

activists in the struggle
for equality,

their question
was the here and now

that speaks to elsewhere,
from wherever it is

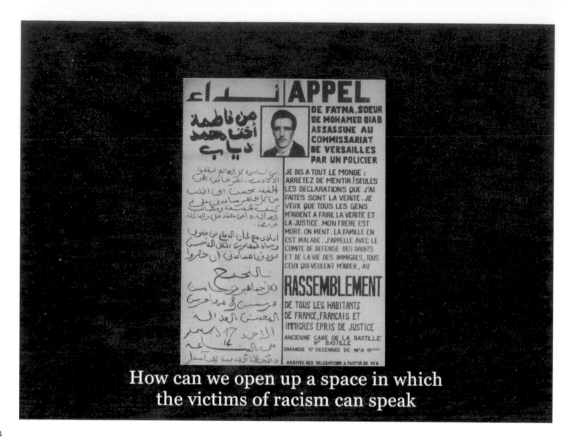

How can we open up a space in which
the victims of racism can speak

beyond the basic humanistic
disapproval of racism

I came to tell you
that I am a man,

APPEL

DE FATNA, SOEUR DE MOHAMED DIAB ASSASSINE AU COMMISSARIAT DE VERSAILLES PAR UN POLICIER

نـــداء
من فاطمة أخت محمد دياب

JE DIS A TOUT LE MONDE : ARRETEZ DE MENTIR ! SEULES LES DECLARATIONS QUE J'AI FAITES SONT LA VERITE . JE VEUX QUE TOUS LES GENS M'AIDENT A FAIRE LA VERITE ET LA JUSTICE . MON FRERE EST MORT . ON MENT . LA FAMILLE EN EST MALADE . J'APPELLE AVEC LE COMITE DE DEFENSE DES DROITS ET DE LA VIE DES IMMIGRES , TOUS CEUX QUI VEULENT M'AIDER , AU

إني أنادي كل العالم ليقفوا الاكاذيب . تصرّحاتي هي الحقيقة محض . إني اطلب من كل الجماهير مساعدتي على كشف الحقيقة ومطالبة العدالة « أخي محمد قتل والعائلة مريضة .

أنادي مع لجان الدفاع عن حقوق وحياة المهاجرين ، لكل الذين يودّون مساعدتي ان يحضروا

RASSEMBLEMENT

DE TOUS LES HABITANTS DE FRANCE, FRANCAIS ET IMMIGRES EPRIS DE JUSTICE

ANCIENNE GARE DE LA BASTILLE
M° BASTILLE

DIMANCHE 17 DECEMBRE DE 14"A 19 HEURES

ARRIVEE DES DELEGATIONS A PARTIR DE 11 H

التجمع لكل جماهير فرنسيين ومهاجرين المحبين العدالة الاحد 17 ديسمبر على الساعة 14 في المحطة القديمة للباستيل

and I demand
to be heard as a man

Bordeaux
from *Les Tiers Idées*, Geneviève Clancy and Philippe Tancelin

*TWO HUNDRED PEOPLE: migrant workers and French
workers. The hall is full, friendly. In the passage
about the administration, the grinder, the fact
that the undocumented workers are being watched by
the authorities all the time, the audience reacts.
They add fuel to the fire. Then comes the scene
of the clubbing. At the far end of the hall
something's happening.*

    *— At the moment when you who play the cop, you
came on stage by the back door ready to pounce on
the Arab man, there was one person in the audience
who was so much into it that he thought it was
really happening. He wanted to jump on stage to
intervene, to punch you in the face. He had to
be restrained. We kept repeating it was a show,
but he replied: 'Yes but it's so much like that
we have to do something about it…'*

    *Some small political groups reproached us
with not having pushed (further) the analysis on
imperialism. The people, the migrants in particular,
didn't let us answer. For nearly two hours they
opposed them. They were defending the play, fighting
every step of the way as if it was theirs.*

It is a cold winter night and you turn up.

    It is cold outside… warmer in the entrance of
the metro… warmer still in the flats where millions
of families gravitate around a television.

*PRESS RELEASE: This afternoon at Versailles police
station, a police sergeant was forced to gun down
an Algerian national who had committed an indecent
assault and was threatening all the officers who
tried to restrain him…*

With you the spectators of our play and with those
who are able to listen to us, we are sharing this
testimony from the sister of Mohamed Diab who was
murdered at Versailles police station:

    'This is not the truth. Our mother was ill

in hospital. My brother Mohamed went to visit her.
He found her weak and went to get her some food,
The nurses tried to stop him and took him to the
office of the hospital's security guard.

'I was informed. When I arrived at the hospital,
the police were already there. I told them to
leave my brother alone, that he hasn't done
anything wrong. They replied: "Your brother is
drunk. We are taking him to the police station."

'They left in a car, and I followed on foot.'

When I arrived at the police station, Mohamed
had his arms in the air, the cops were searching
him, insulting him. I told them: "Leave my brother
alone, he's not done anything." They threw me out,
shouting: "Beat it, scum."

I stayed outside and through the window I could
see everything. Mohamed took a chair as if he
wanted to protect himself from the blows that were
raining down from all sides. The cops took chairs
too, and there was an exchange of blows, then it
was calm again. Mohamed sat down facing Sergeant
Marquet and said:

"You'd like to kill me, right?"

"Yes, I'll kill you, scum of the earth, I'll
kill you!"

Mohamed got up, moved one step forward. Marquet
took his submachine gun and shot twice. Mohamed did
a spin then collapsed. That's it, that's the truth,
that's the truth.' (29 November 1972).

On stage, motionless, a comrade repeats Fatna
Diab's words:

'That's the truth, that's the truth, and we
investigated.'

We will speak for ourselves
and for those who cannot speak

We start with them and their idea
of a "theatrical newspaper"

A newspaper unfolded
over a theatre stage,

where resistance emerges
through confrontation

Performance without theatre,
or theatre without performance?

à Barbès

SAMEDI 20 OCTOBRE

20 h 30

à l'initiative du
Comité **M. Diab** et du
**Mouvement des Travailleurs
Arabes**

T

" **ÇA TRAVAILL**

ÇA FERME S

PIECE ECRIT

PAR DES TR

LA PIECE SERA S

-entrée gratuite-

EATRE

CENTRE 8

8 rue Porte de
Buc

- VERSAILLES-

, ÇA TRAVAILLE

GUEULE"

MONTÉE ET JOUÉE
VAILLEURS IMMIGRÉS

VIE D'UN DEBAT

comité Diab
versailles

M4 *

20 11

✕ Α1

ΠΑΙΔΙΑ

300

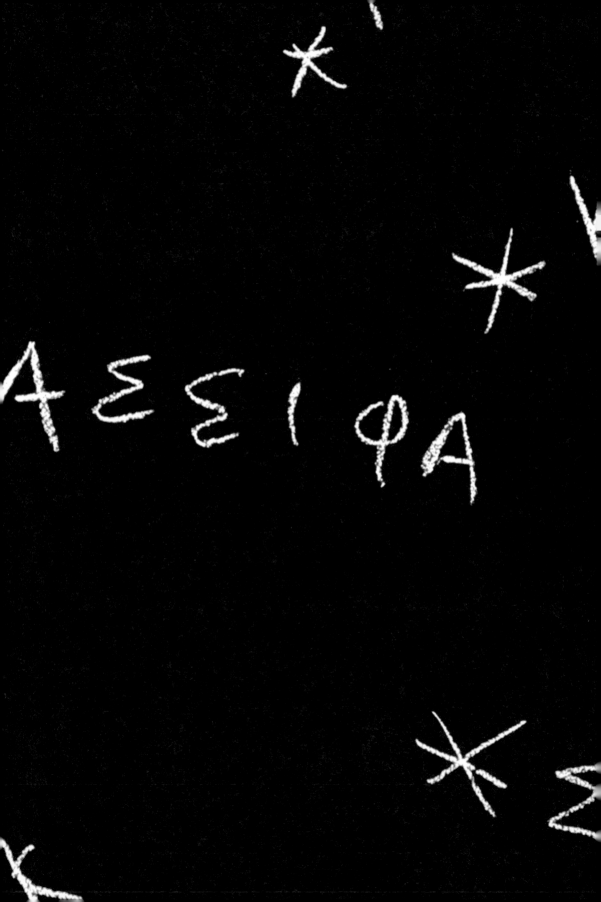

The Movement for Arab Workers and the Assifa Theatre Company

Abdellali Hajjat

– Djilali: *Yadhitou, yadhitou! Yadhitou, yadhitou! Yadhitou, yadhitou! Al passpor yadhitou!*[1]

– Another character: Explain *kifach* [how] *yadhitou!*

– Fifteen days ago, I'm walking in the street...

– Another character: *Ahdhar m'aya bil'arbiya!* [speak to me in Arabic!]

– Djilali: *Ya ouildi* [my son], if you want to go to Europe, to France especially... if you don't want people to be racist, you got to speak their language. That's why the caïd he says to me 'you got to speak French', so I learnt and I speak...[2] [laughter and clapping in the room]

– Another character: He's right, he's right...

– Djilali: So I'm walking in the streets of my village. You know Mohammed? The caïd's son? His father is the caïd. Me, Djilali, my father, he's a peasant. He was done like that [gesture with his hand], they take his land from him, it's for the king... The king, he's poor... [laughter] And me, I was in senior school. They kick me out. And Mohammed, the caïd's son, as usual, he's at university like all the caïd's sons... [laughter] He's doing medicine, *tbib... douctour...* The other day I'm walking in the street, like that, like usual, on my way... home...

– Another character: On your way to the café!

– Djilali: Home!

– Another character: The café!

– Djilali: Like all the Moroccans, unemployed... [laughter and clapping] And he sees me fifty metres away... the caïd's son, he's running behind me: 'Ah Djilali, ah Djilali, come here!' '*Yallatif, yallatif*!' say... 'What's up *ya sayid*?' He says, 'My father, he wants to see you.' The caïd, he wants to see me? Why? I don't do politics... [laughter] 'No, no, no,' he says, 'this time it's not to put you in prison'... [laughter] 'it's to help you go to Europe!' Yiiiii! I tell him, *'Me abourab!* Five years I've been running for the passport, *walou!* I only got my birth certificate...' [laughter] He tells me, 'This time I promise you... one hundred per cent guarantee, like watches... it's going to work...' Me, I say, 'What do I do for them to give me the passport?' He tells me 'You know... you've seen the Americans... tourists...' The Americans are always here... They take everything... [laughter] The Americans they want a gazelle.[3] They came to the caïd. So the caïd's son he tells me 'if you bring the gazelle, my father, he gives you the passport.' I immediately thumb a lift *m'a* [with] the walkers... towards the Black March[4]... *Dakhlat fi Sahra* there... [laughter] I find the cousins, I arrive at night in the douar... Yiiiii! The dogs! Ob ob ob! All the cousins they come out, the little ones, the big ones, the middle ones, all... [laughter] 'What're you doing in the village? It's been ten years since we've seen you, *ya* Djilali, what's up?' Ah *qoutalhoum* 'I have a big story' and I tell them the story of the caïd. 'Ah', they say, 'don't worry, tonight you have a gazelle and you go to Marrakech to get your papers.' Marrakech, the next day, with my gazelle... I arrive in the morning... I arrive at the caïd's office... Toc, toc, toc... Hop, the guards and all, they let me in with my gazelle... The Americans are there... Check, check like the pictures of the man there... [in the hall] [laughter] with the gazelle... And I give it to him, he's all happy, he hugs me, 'you, Djilali, you're a real son of the desert, that's why we want the *sahra*...' [laughter and clapping] Immediately I give the pictures, tof, tof, [noise of the rubber stamp], the passport, and also a bag of American flour and a tin of oil for the starving family... [laughter and clapping] Me: Goodbye *ya* Dole! Goodbye *ya* Misery! Goodbye the café that refuses to do credit! I no longer stay here! The cousins who work at Citroën, they come back for the summer with cars... with blonde girls and roses and everything... And me, what am I doing here? The café and home, fed up with that! Tonight I'm off, for France! *Wallah!* [5]

59

Al Assifa, untitled, unknown place between November 1975 and March 1976.

In this humorous sketch by the Al Assifa Theatre Company, the main character, Djilali, is a young Moroccan, uneducated, thrown out of senior school, and unemployed, whose days are spent going back and forth between the local café and home.[6] He represents a typical figure in France in the nineteen-seventies, the 'immigrant worker'. At odds with the miserabilist view of the immigrant worker usually conveyed by the mainstream French media and often by some political movements, Al Assifa offered an entirely different story: a critical and popular vision, both amusing and satirical, anchored in the daily life of North African immigrants, and rarely made public. Through a dialogue lasting a few minutes, the actors of Al Assifa dealt with the question of social misery in Morocco, the corruption and the relations of subordination with the caïd and the inequalities that undermined the country: political repression against political opponents[7] ('it's not to put you in prison'), relations between emigrants and non-emigrants (the 'cars' and the 'blonde girls'), and United States' imperialism ('they take everything!'). Even the question of the Western Sahara (the 'Black March') is analysed as a form of colonialism.

These were the thorny subjects that the Al Assifa company tackled with humour and lightness, which fitted with a far-left political discourse, critical of the long-standing power structures of the country of emigration as much as of those in the country of immigration. In this sense, the Al Assifa Company was part of the 'momentum of May '68' that corresponds with what Michel de Certeau called an extensive 'speaking'. May '68 was that crucial historical moment in the history of France when all the social outcasts – workers, women, students, immigrants, homosexuals, lesbians, and self-identified members of oppressed minorities – rose up against the logics of domination by the social and political institutions. The immigrant workers took part in that new social movement. Some even ended up being expelled from the French territory for daring to raise their head and protest against the inequalities they were subjected to.[8] If May '68 was a decisive historical episode in the journey of the Al Assifa company's actors, unfinished decolonisation was equally decisive. Al Assifa was an outgrowth of the Movement for Arab Workers (MTA) that claimed the legacy of the Pan-Arab revolutionaries and developed a virulent criticism of the 'reactionary' elites in power in Arab countries.[9]

In order to understand the Al Assifa company, it is necessary to revisit the MTA and the role the theatre played in the mobilisation of immigrant workers in France.

PROFILES OF POLITICAL EMIGRANTS

It is impossible to understand the engagement of the MTA if one doesn't revisit the conditions of emigration of its founders. Their emigration was anomic, in the sense that it was motivated by social reasons connected to individual trajectories of rupture with the established social order or by political reasons, especially the repression of the Tunisian regime. The profile of the MTA militants was similar to that of the pioneers of the Étoile nord-africaine,[10] analysed by Abdelmalek Sayad[11] with the concept of jayah which means in Algerian Arabic 'the one who is lost, gone astray, who no longer is on the right path'. Used in a pejorative way within Arab families, the concept was understood differently by Sayad. His aim was to understand the position and political trajectory of political militants outside the main population. Their political engagement was explained by the idea of rupture, a delicate position that produced a greater sensibility to the relations of domination and a will to liberate oneself from the social constraints of the dominant order. The routes of the MTA militants illustrate first a decisive break with the traditional social order of North African societies. At this time, the traditional emigrant was a married man leaving in order to support his family and the wider community. The MTA militants broke with this, emigrating as single men in order to escape conservative restraint. Second, they marked a rupture with the emerging national order. The MTA militants were the children of independence. Some of them actively or modestly took part in the war of liberation, especially the Algerians.[12] But by the end of the sixties, they found themselves having broken with the nationalist ranks, for various reasons and according to national political contexts. The Tunisian founders of the MTA were Marxist nationalists, close to the far-left movement Perspectives tunisiennes, which was quite influential among the young citizens of Tunis. But, at the time of the war in June 1967, there was a disengagement from the national agenda that Perspectives tunisiennes decided to favour for an international agenda focused around the Palestinian struggle.[13]

The MTA members were militants shaped by a pan-Arabic and Marxist national conscience, who found themselves forced to emigrate for political or personal reasons. It was no coincidence that the Palestinian cause was the first battlefield on which they rallied in France, particularly after Black September, the event which initiated the creation of Comités Palestine in France.[14] Some of them had become politicised in their country of origin and some in France, within the Fédération de France du FLN. Others picked it up as they went along, especially within the Maoist far-left movement Gauche prolétarienne (GP). This alliance was made possible because the GP had a clear agenda with regards to reaching immigrant workers who were considered to be the most exploited and, consequently, to 'naturally' form the avant-garde of the proletarian revolution. The Arab militants' attraction to GP at the end of the sixties and beginning of the seventies can be explained by two factors: the first (a sociological reference) shows how the politicised workers rallied with and right beside those French people who were not like the others; the second

(the radical anti-Zionist position of GP) enables us to understand how easy it was to work in common with the students of the Comités Palestine. Contrary to the Trotskyists' position of 'critical support', GP was totally in line with the strategy of the PLO.[15] Besides, the field work of GP (leaflets, protest marches, etc.) gave them a 'good reputation' from the point of view of the Arab militants of Comités Palestine. Gradually, the political agenda of the Comités Palestine changed as they began to 'follow the mass movement', and not only to support the Palestinian struggle, but also to give expression and political organisation to the new figure of the immigrant worker. They were given an opportunity with the Djellali Ben Ali case.

On Wednesday, 27 October 1971, Djellali Ben Ali, a fifteen-year-old teenage boy of Algerian nationality, was killed by a gunshot to the head fired by Daniel Pigot, a twenty-nine-year-old delivery man, at 53 rue de la Goutte d'Or (18th arrondissement, Paris).[16] The case highlighted the racial tensions rife in the quarter, actively encouraged by far-right militia like Ordre nouveau or Comités de défense de la République (CDR). Within this context a mobilisation was called for by the militants of Comités Palestine from the neighbourhood (among them 'Sélim' Najeh, Saïd and Faouzia Bouziri, Mohamed 'Mokhtar' Bachiri, Majid Daboussi) and Secours rouge in the 18th arrondissement.[17] It was supported by people living in the neighbourhood as well as socially and politically committed intellectuals (in particular Michel Foucault, Claude Mauriac, Gilles Deleuze, Michèle Manceaux, Jean-Claude Passeron and Jean-Paul Sartre) who founded the Comité Djellali.[17] The support of intellectuals and Father Gallimardet and Pastor Hedrich from the church in the area (who put at the Committee's disposal the Maison verte of rue Marcadet and the Hall Saint-Bruno, where the committee room was organised) and the campaign of political awareness led by Comités Palestine contributed to the media impact of the case and an important mobilisation. This reached its peak on 7 November with a protest march of about 4,000 people in the streets of Barbès.[18]

It was in this type of mobilisation that connections and at times conflicts were woven between Arab militants, far-left French support committees, and those coming from social Christianity and the immigrant population. May 1968 gave the opportunity for political encounters that seem improbable if not impossible but for the inspiration of those events. The confrontation between those various actors sheds a light on the limits of convergence between different social and political milieux, a tension that led the MTA to consider its action around the concept of autonomy.

POLITICAL AUTONOMY

The commitment to the immigrant cause took on the double logics of autonomy and alliance in a political sector where the political resources of all were shared. For the Maoists, the Arab militants (students and workers), who had high social capital at their disposal within the Arab community, were 'couriers' in charge of raising awareness in the North African populations, and were often, due to illiteracy, lack of education and political awareness, reticent to their political discourse. The Arab militants put their knowledge of Arabic and the immigrant world to good use. For them, an alliance with the French was necessary in order to access resources of which they were deprived: the financing of militant activities, the experience of different modes of action, the media, and the ability to mobilise people over abuses of workers' rights. A convergence of interests was established in order to create a relatively solid alliance, until a series of events saw cracks appear.

In reality, the MTA was a novelty in the history of the French working class. It was the first time Arab workers tried to organise themselves autonomously, and it responded to the *de facto* exclusion of immigrants from trade union power. Their demands were scarcely taken on board, if not openly negated, by the trade union machinery, hence their closeness with Maoists who were 'established'.[19] The immigrant workers' rights were denied first of all because of their status as foreigners. Their exclusion from the political and trade union world was ratified by French legislation which enforced a separation between the national and the foreign. But that exclusion was also due to the practices of the trade union machinery, which showed a total blindness when faced with the reality of the immigrant workers. As French companies used immigrant workers to put pressure on 'French' workers in terms of wages and working conditions, big unions considered immigrant workers a divisive factor. Moreover, the trade unions only conceived of working class struggles within the framework of the factory: the class struggle stopped at the factory door. But the Arab workers were also affected by housing problems and racism, and for that reason they broadened the field of class struggle. Their oppression was experienced at the same time in the factory, in the café, at home, and in the street. The trade unions did not seem to grasp that new phenomenon.

In addition, it was taken for granted that immigrant workers would go 'back home' after a few years. This myth, that the Arab workers would return to their countries of origin, contributed to giving priority to the protection and advancement of the rights and freedoms for the national worker under attack from the management. The organisation of Arab workers in France can then be understood as one of the first most obvious or visible signs of the will of Arab immigrants to settle on French territory – and therefore as one of the first cracks appearing in the myth of the return and the order of emigration. Consequently, the existence of an organisation of Arab workers radically subverted both the national order when it broke with the dogma of 'political neutrality' expected of the foreigner and the trade union order that had remained deaf to the specific demands of the immigrants that also went beyond the factory.

Moreover, the existence of the MTA exposed flaws in the control of immigration by the consular representations of the countries of origin. The power of the Amicales (associations) was directly contested, disrupting the relations between immigrant populations and countries of origin. The Amicales were supposed to be associations of immigrants organised by their home countries, such as the 'Amicale of the Algerians in France'. In reality, they were organised by diplomatic institutions to keep their nationals under control. They were also infiltrated by spies who were reporting to internal security forces in Algeria or Morocco about political activities conducted by their nationals in France. The action of the MTA led to a far-reaching questioning of the use of state of origin to manage immigration. The Arab workers were no longer 'traded' between states, but spoke up directly to claim their autonomy in the face of the various bodies trying to manage them: the French state, French trade-unions, Arab states, and Arab political parties.

The question of autonomy was also central for the Comités Palestine. At the congress where the MTA was founded (June 1972), the Arab militants considered they were not autonomous enough, and that they were in fact controlled by French intellectuals. In the political texts of Comités Palestine, for the MTA the term 'autonomy' was rarely precisely defined. A kind of implicit agreement on its definition existed, but it remained vague for the people on the outside. It was therefore essential to clarify that notion in order to comprehend all that was at stake around them, since autonomy was a claim in itself for the Arab militants. It was supposed to be the solution to their problems but precisely what problems was it supposed to solve?

The testimonies of experiences of struggle on the part of Arab workers during the Founding Congress of the MTA confirmed that the absence of autonomy was detrimental to the success of the strikes in factories. The challenge was to be found in the question of decision making, political control and power of the Arab workers, and in the demand for *political and organisational autonomy* that was close to the principle of self-determination. The Arab workers of the MTA had already had enough experience of power being taken by the trade union confederations, and believed that the decisions had to be taken first by the people concerned. The problem was particularly acute in factories where an overwhelming majority of North African skilled workers were employed, which was the case for almost all the workers gathered at the congress. Political autonomy did not mean political separatism in the eyes of the MTA militants. It was not a question of putting an end to the existence of the committees of struggle in the workshops in which one met with French workers as well as workers of other nationalities, but to clear a political space for the aspirations of Arab workers to be voiced, in order to satisfy their claims. In other words, the Arab workers would have more political weight if they were self-organised to find solutions to their own problems, but this was not taken into account by French trade unions. So, the claim for political and organisational autonomy was the outcome of the political exclusion of the immigrants, as brought about by French social law and by the practice of trade union confederations. If the latter had met the expectations of the Arab workers, there is no doubt they would have integrated into the trade union frame-work, which in some instances was the case.

CULTURAL AUTONOMY

The second aspect of autonomy is of a *cultural* nature. Faced by the ideology of integration-assimilation, the Arab workers demanded cultural autonomy. Some of the claims that surfaced in the years

1970–71, such as the right to organise the celebration of Eid Al Kebir, or the right to teach Arabic, could seem insignificant, but they structurally subverted the state conception of immigration, with its emphasis on the natural integration of migrants into the national community. From the point of view of the state, if a foreigner intends to settle in France they are required to integrate into the culture of the majority community, on the principle that cultural homogeneity is essential to social cohesion. To maintain cultural claims and resist this injunction calls into question the idea of the 'French-style model of integration'. For the militants of the MTA, belonging to the Arab nation was perceived as a way toward cultural unification that went hand in hand with political unity. To obtain that unity, it was necessary to face up to the threats of 'cultural extinction' through the teaching of Arabic and the history of the Arab world. The social and political issue at stake was the capacity of the immigrants to define themselves culturally, but that capacity tended to be largely compromised by the power that the injunction to integrate carried. Cultural autonomy was also a profound refusal of state categorisations for which 'immigrant' was synonymous with 'worker'. By appending the adjective 'Arab', the whole concept of the politics of immigration, conceived as an impassive management of the migratory flux founded on nationalities, was questioned.

It was in the framework of this cultural autonomy that the Al Assifa company was created. The idea for the company had been germinating since November 1970, when Comités Palestine had offered to set up a 'revolutionary theatre'. The proposition became reality during the hunger strike of the undocumented immigrants of Ménilmontant in Paris in May 1973.[20] Despite the success of the strike, given all the inconveniences of hunger strikes and the limits of traditional methods of action (pamphlets, posters, etc.), the question of what was effective political action was raised: 'How to explain the struggle of the immigrants by other means than giving out leaflets?' the militants pondered. So, the Assifa company was created and the first play Ça travaille, ça travaille et ça ferme sa gueule (One works, works, and shuts up) collectively developed. Farid Aïchoune, Heddi Akkari, Mokhtar Bachiri, Ahmed Bouraka (alias 'Djillali'), Fawzia Bouziri, Mustapha Charchari, Geneviève Clancy, Kheira, Ali Majri (alias 'Ali Clichy'), Phillipe Tancelin, and Salem Younsi comprised the company. For them, theatre became the means to efficiently raise political awareness. 'If you come to present your life on stage, but with humour, people have a laugh, and then they think' – because the immigrants identify with the scenes. They clearly were also in line with writers like Aimé Césaire and Kateb Yacine, the latter writing a play on immigration, Mohamed prends ta valise (Mohamed take your suitcase) in the mid-seventies.

The script, largely improvised at the beginning, makes a mockery of the lack of space in rooms, the illiteracy at home, the relations between immigrants and non-immigrants. The theatre group was conceived as an efficient means of struggle, which overcame the problems of trying to politicise an immigrant population often lacking literacy skills and extensive political knowledge. Unlike meetings or pamphlets, theatre reached a wide audience of all types and ages and could distil political messages that, generally, provoked laughs and clapping in the audience, as the sketch on the 'gazelle for the Americans' illustrates. Besides, a theatre play didn't require enormous financial investment at the beginning, and they themselves were the actors. With Mokhtar Bachiri as 'leader', they even received help from Geneviève Clancy's husband, Jacques (an actor), Daniel Deferre and Pierre Rival. With the money raised from collections at the end of each performance, they bought a sound system and rehearsed in the Hall Saint-Bruno in Paris's 18th arrondissement. The company benefited from the logistical assistance of Claude Floreau, who was close to the Comité de Défense de la vie et des droits des travailleurs immigrés (CDVDTI) and trade unionists from the Confédération Française Démocratique du Travail (CFDT), who lent the hall of the CFDT branch in Myrha Street at the heart of 'La Goutte d'Or'.

To successfully complete the work of 'raising awareness', Al Assifa made use of a very important element of immigrant popular culture. For them, theatre was not perceived as an elitist art reserved for season ticket holders of prestigious Parisian theatres, but as a form of oral art close to the traditional 'al Halqa' or the *moussem*.[21] This political art used the social connections of the immigrant community mainly concentrated in some neighbourhoods in Paris or in Marseille, but also in the militant networks. Al Assifa went touring in the militant milieu of the seventies: Fête de Lutte Ouvrière, Maison de la Jeunesse et de la Culture (MJC), Bonneuil, ESSEC Cergy-Pontoise, MJC Houilles, Boulogne, Chalon-sur-Saône, Lyon, Grenoble, MJC Versailles, Ivry, Puteaux, Bordeaux, and the Fête de la rencontre Français-Immigrés that took place on 10 and 11 June 1978 at the Chelles cultural centre. The company also did many performances in support of the workers' strike at the LIP factory (28 September 1973) and the sustained strike of the foyers Sonacotra (1974–1980).

'ART FOR ART' OR 'ART FOR POLITICS'?

However, conversations held with the militants, as well as archive material, show that the creation of the Al Assifa company was symptomatic of a loss of impetus in the ranks of the MTA: a 'lack of political perspectives' as well as the shrinking of the militants' core – those prepared to sacrifice their studies and their work for political engagement.[22] '[We formed Al Assifa] because we were struggling a bit with endless activism in the streets. We also wanted the cultural

frameworks to exist.' In 1975, at the very moment that Al Assifa experienced an important development, the demobilisation and dispersal of the MTA militants connected with the struggles of Arab workers was apparent. The play *Ça travaille, ça travaille et ça ferme sa gueule* became a big success: between May and July 1975, it was performed fifteen times all over France.

Starting from nothing, the MTA militants succeeded in setting up a truly professional company, the stated political motivations of which, however, became less and less clear. At the MTA national congress of 13–14 July 1975, one of Al Assifa's founders, Mokhtar, didn't hesitate to denounce the distancing of militant concerns from the company. 'The cultural activities that have started all over the place in France performed by Al Assifa from the struggles of the immigrants have turned into independent plays cut off from the reality of immigrant workers' daily life in the neighbourhood and factory.' The question put was this: What conception of culture has the MTA adopted? Was it art for art, or art in the service of political engagement?

The problem was all the more difficult for the militants facing up to attempts of political appropriation. Zouhair and other MTA militants from Grenoble had used 'the form of expression through sketches' while going through Grenoble's various neighbourhoods (MJC, social centres, etc.), but in March 1973 the socialist mayor of Grenoble created the Théâtre Populaire Maghrébin (TPM), 'with the purpose of channelling the revolutionary actions of the masses', and gave it significant resources: two permanent Moroccan employees and a budget of 10,000 French francs. The theatre, as a means of expression, offered the MTA militants new openings that contrasted or coincided with the lack of political perspectives. For Saïd Bouziri, 'if there's cash (Socialist Party, Mauroy, Deferre), we must pinch it. For us, culture is the

65

first struggle, a struggle for expression but also a political springboard.'[23]

Besides, the 'Amicales' associations of the countries of origin also invested in the cultural sector. In Guebwiller, the Amicale des Marocains en France organised evening entertainments with national stars quite successfully. All those elements made Bachiri even more suspicious: 'We shouldn't forget that the authorities are trying to take us over but don't try in any way to develop an Arab culture. Therefore, we face the politics of state funding, knowing that immigrants 'don't party for the sake of partying, but use parties as a form of struggle.' Following the discussions of the cultural front, the MTA decided to remain vigilant of 'cultural forms that can be appropriated', namely theatre and songs but also literacy teaching that the government didn't intend to leave to the Arab 'lefties', and the dangers of entering councils' structures. To reinforce the position of the MTA, the national congress decided to set up an 'Arab cultural association in France' (Law 1901), a monthly release of music tapes (one side with information, the other side with songs)

and the constitution of a *moussem* (suggested by Djilali Kamal). But the decisions taken during that congress had no effect on the functioning of the company. The gradual autonomy of the company from the MTA materialised with the creation of the play *La vie de château (The castle life)*.

In the militant space, political dispositions depreciated, or at least no longer brought about the positive change expected. The success of the Al Assifa company had lasted several years, and the MTA militants were responsible for the first free radio stations for immigrants: Radio Soleil in Paris, Radio Gazelle in Marseille. These radio stations should be considered as the continuation of the cultural autonomy project by other means and were very important for the birth of a new political movement at the end of the 1970s, including Maghrebi immigrants' children's groups such as Rock against Police (Paris) and Zaama d'Banlieue (Lyon), which opened a new era in the politics of immigration in France.

Translated by Catherine Petit & Paul Buck

1

'I got it! I got it! I got it! I got it! I got it! The passport, I got it.' Having a passport was considered a privilege in Morocco until the early 1990s.

2

Caïd is a civil servant appointed by the state to represent it in smaller communities. Traditionally, the caïd belonged to a distinguished family.

3

Slang for young woman.

4

The Black March is a play on words referring the Green March, a mass demonstration organised by the Moroccan government to force Spain to hand over the disputed province of Spanish Sahara to Morocco.

5

Yallatif, yallatif! [Oh my God!], ya sayid [Sir], me abourab [my God], walou! [nothing!], m'a [with], Dakhlat fi Sahra [I went into the desert], qoutalhoum [I told them], sahra [desert], Wallah! [I swear!]

6

Al Assifa means 'storm' in Arabic and is also the name of the armed wing of the Palestinian liberation movement 'Fatah'.

7

In the 1970's, thousands of left-wing activists were jailed in Moroccan prisons.

8

In May '68, immigrants were expelled for their political activities, and in order to defend 'public order' political activity for immigrants was illegal. In 1972, Saïd Bouziri, a founder of MTA, and his wife Faouzia went on hunger strike to protest arbitrary deportations.

9

The Mouvement des Travailleurs Arabes (MTA – Movement of Arab Workers) was founded in 1972 in Paris by Arab and French activists, some affiliated or close to the Gauche Prolétarienne, and many members of the 'Palestine Commitees', including Bouziri and Mokhtar.

10

The Étoile nord-africaine was the first Maghrebi, mostly Algerian, anti-colonial movement, born in the context of immigration in France. The profile of the first anti-colonial activists was the one of the jayah according to Sayad.

11

Abdelmalek Sayad (1933–1998) was an Algerian sociologist considered to be the best ethnographer of Algerian immigration in France. See *The Suffering of the Immigrant* (Polity Press, 2004).

12

The War of Liberation, or the Algerian Revolution (1954–1962), as it was described by the National Liberation Front (FLN), led to Algeria gaining independence from France.

13

The June War of 1967, 1967 Arab–Israeli War, or Third Arab–Israeli War, was fought between 5–10 June 1967 by Israel and the neighbouring states of the United Arab Republic (Egypt), Jordan, and Syria.

14

Black September, 1970, was the attack on Palestinians in Jordan by the army of King Hussein. The Palestinian presence in Jordan had become a threat to his rule.

15

The concept of critical support means that one supports the cause of the organisation but criticises some aspects of its discourse or strategy. Until 1988 the PLO's position was for a binational state with equal rights for all citizens.

16

Goutte d'Or is a part of the 18th arrondissement that had a large community of North African workers. Today it is going through a process of gentrification.

17

In 1970, with the help of Jean-Paul Sartre, Gauche Prolétarienne had formed Secours rouge (Red Aid) a prisoner's aid and anti-fascist organisation.

18

Barbès is a famous Maghrebi neighbourhood of the 18th arrondissement of Paris close to Goutte d'Or.

19

'Établissement' was the practice of middle or upper class activists working in factories to politically agitate. See Robert Linhart, *L'Établi* (Éditions de Minuit, 1978).

20

In response to the Marcellin-Fontanet circulars (1972) which discriminated against workers without housing or work, a hunger strike was called, and supported by the local priest.

21

Al Halqa is a traditional North African form of storytelling, narrated to a surrounding crowd in open-air spaces. Moussem is a big fair mixing forms of artistic expression and discussion.

22

By the mid-1970s the idea of an imminent revolution after May '68 had vanished among left-wing activists in France.

23

Pierre Mauroy, Mayor of Lille, and Gaston Deferre Mayor of Marseilles, both served as ministers in Mitterrand's government in 1981.

COLLECTIF ASSIFA

G^{pe} SALVE   G. CLANCY   707 36 03 ou 033 03

P. TANCELIN

MOKTAR & HABIB

307 28 68

les LEZARDS

636 II 28

BENDIR DÉCHAÎNÉ

307 28 68

radio ASSIFA

200 4 ᴔ 50

centre de recherche & documentation

35 Rue Stéphenson Paris 75018 Tél: 606 15 6

Théâtre...............Musique....................Poésie......
..............Radio.....................Information..........
.Poésie..........Théâtre.....................Radio.........
.......Documentation..............Musique.........Poésie.

COLLECTIF

69

ASSIFA

PRESENTE

.......Théâtre.........Musique.......Poésie.......Radio.......

Information.................Documentation..............Théâtre......

An interview with Mokhtar, one of the founders of Al Assifa company
from *Les Tiers Idées*, Geneviève Clancy and Philippe Tancelin

'*Ça travaille…* is a theatrical collage set to
illustrate the struggle of the immigrant workers.
It was the third or fourth attempt to do militant
theatre. It corresponded to a cultural resolution,
a will to fight a battle, as theatre was going
hand in hand with what we were doing at the time,
the struggles in which we were engaged.

'Our first attempt was a play on Palestine.
We relied on a worker who had a bit of experience
and he began writing a play. We wanted the students
to help us set it up. With them we met people
in the Cité.[1] They criticised the content of the
play with "Marxist critiques". The discourse of
the play was not very political. Up against the
reaction of the students, we decided to rely
solely on ourselves. Faced with the attitude of
the intellectuals, the worker who had written it
refused, as if it was a question of pride, any
modification to his text. That's how the first
project came to an end. The second project was
in the heat of the hunger strikes.[2] It took
place in Saint-Maur. One of the workers offered
to write the text. A group was formed, with the
idea of stimulating the setting up of a cultural
organisation. Some volunteers arrived, with
various and varied ambitions: music, cinema,
theatre, and more…

'As far as theatre was concerned, there were
to be two reasons why it failed. One worker wrote
a text to be performed. In reality it was a story,
a tale that proved impossible for us to adapt for
the stage, because we had no knowledge in that
field. On top of that, the working sessions were
weighed down by ideas and agendas that were very
loaded. Each time we met we talked about music,
cinema, etc., and theatre, which was our project,
ended up being side-lined. Finally the third attempt
failed. There were only the hunger strikers of
Ménilmontant involved in the whole production that
took place during the strike. Some people chose

the sketches that were to be performed during the
celebration for the victory of the undocumented of
Ménilmontant. They were ready but, in the programme
of the day, when they were supposed to perform,
a troupe of Arab students was set to go on stage
too. As soon as they arrived with their gear, the
workers, intimidated by their skills, backed off
for fear of being less proficient. So, in the end,
they didn't perform.

'Then came Lip.[3] I was among the delegates
representing the migrant workers in their struggle,
meeting a delegation from Lip. After a debate
on our conditions of life and our struggle, they
invited us to come to their place, to talk about
it. Their demand was: "Come with a cultural
agenda, whatever it is, around which the discussions
can evolve."

   'So some people from the Ménilmontant group
gathered, accompanied by two or three Arab
militants. We decided to create some kind of
theatre collage based on our struggle — collective
discussions, rough drafts of the scenes. We agreed
on three typed-up pages that we were going to
perform, to give life to. We left for Lip,
accompanied by some French militants and some
professional theatre people.
   'That's how Ça travaille, ça travaille et ça
ferme sa gueule was born.'

1
Théâtre de la Cité is the theatre
on the international students
campus in Paris.

2
Mokhtar refers to the hunger strike
in protest against the Marcellin-
Fontanet circulars, 1972.

3
Lip was a watch factory located
in the East of France, close to
the Swiss border. Following a strike
against a secret restructuring plan,
the factory became a symbol of a
successful occupation: the workers
decided to keep making watches
and to sell them themselves.
Their slogan was: we make them,
we sell them, we pay ourselves.

Then there was
and I fought with th

ακή, (ἀστική) δημοκρατία στήν Ἑλλάδα, ὁ Παναγούλης θά προ-
αγγίσει τόν Μαρξισμό, μέσ' ἀπό ἕνα μηχανισμό ἀσυγκράτητο.
Ἀλλά πρός τό παρόν, καί προπαντός μέχρι τώρα, ἔκανε καλά πού
ώθησε αὐτές τίς τάσεις γιά μιάν ἐντελῶς ὀρθολογική — καί ἐπο-
ένως προβληματική καί ἀπαρχή — ἀντίληψη τῆς κοινωνίας. Στόν
γώνα του γιά τήν Ἐλευθερία, δηλαδή τήν παραδειακή Δημο-
ρατία, ἐκεῖνο πού ὑπῆρξε βασικά καί ἀντικειμενικά ὀρθολογι-
τικό, ἦταν ἀκριβῶς ἡ, ἐκ μέρους του ἄρνηση τοῦ ὀρθολογισμοῦ.
Ἡ τάση του νά ἐμπνέεται ἀπ' τήν ὑπεράσπιση μιᾶς conditio sine
ua non τόσο αὐταπόδεικτης, ὅσο καί ἀπόλυτης. Ὅσοιοι ζῆσανε
ά χρόνια τῆς ἀντίστασης στήν Ἰταλία, γνωρίζουν αὐτή τή μορφή
ῆς ἄκαμπτης βεβαιότητας πού κάνει πολύτιμο ὅ,τι ἀγγίζει. Ἡ
ιότη, ἡ ἐμμονη ἰδέα τοῦ Παναγούλη, πού βασίζεται ἐπάνω σέ μιά
ογική ὄχι διαλεκτική, εἶναι μιά ἀπό κεῖνες τίς μορφές ὑπαρξης
αί ἀγώνα πού ἡ ἱστορία πλάθει μέ τά ἴδια της τά χέρια προσδίδον-
άς τους μιά στοιχειώδη τελειότητα.

Π. Π. ΠΑΖΟΛΙΝΙ
(Μετ. Μιχ. Πασχάλη)

e Resistance
eapons of poetry

2

On Bearing Witness: Conversation between Bouchra Khalili, Phillipe Tancelin and Alexandre Kauffmann

BOUCHRA
How did you feel about being on the film set and about appearing in the film?

PHILIPPE
It may surprise you, but as one of the last surviving members of Al Assifa this raised the question of the historical responsibility of the testimony, which I can frame as follows: To whom do I bear witness? Do I bear witness for what I've experienced? Or do I bear witness of the relationship I lived with those who were also witnesses and protagonists of the same experiment? Do I bear witness to something broader than the specific moment in which I was a protagonist and a witness? To put it more simply, I must first ask myself: what can be said through my voice?

I then quickly had the feeling that the missing ones, the absentees, were coming back, and that they had come to bear witness at the very moment that I was representing them. Second, what moved me was the atmosphere of the film set: this former factory, these young people, the static shots that you had prepared in which I could perceive the dialectic of the absence/presence that was resonating in the present.

BOUCHRA
You're more than a witness: you are a protagonist re-appearing in the contemporary moment.

PHILIPPE
I had acted in the context of a collective that we had created. But on your set, it was different. I had to ask myself: what is the authority of my voice in the context of a testimony?

BOUCHRA
In the context of the shooting, your words were contextualised: you were performing words that had been written by a collective. And the book from which these words originated was shown in the same scenes. So I did not see it as a testimony, but rather as the persistence of history resonating in the present.

PHILIPPE
Absolutely. It was a contextualised and factual speech. The text I performed was written a long time ago. And the protagonists who are no longer here were brought back into the now.

BOUCHRA
You were saying that in the moment of the performance, the absentees were with you?

PHILIPPE
They were there. I could feel it very strongly. But again, that was also to do with the atmosphere: this beautiful light and the immensity of the space, the great concentration of the visual apparatus: one table, four characters and a few photos. The extreme simplicity was overwhelming. And in this the sense of their presence impressed me a lot. I saw these young Athenians holding pictures of us on their faces. It was like a reverse-shot. The absentees were suddenly there, but the photos also formed an image of the past like a screen projecting onto the present.

BOUCHRA
Would you say the absentees were like
ghosts – a haunting presence?

PHILIPPE
Not really. To me, they were a real presence
that was suddenly part of our present-
time. They emerged into the atmosphere
in which you had immersed us, but without
any nostalgic connotations. I had the
feeling that whilst those written words
were being performed an imaginary screen
was suddenly formed that burst the gap
between the past and the present. I also
had the feeling that the sudden appearance
of the absentees suggested a trial was
taking place on the screen – the screen
onto which the past was being projected.

ALEXANDRE
You use the word 'trial': it's a very strong
word. It implies that the visual apparatus
formed by the table and the photos
prepared for a judgement of the past.
And as if you were summoned to testify.

PHILIPPE
You can say it like that. I mean more like
being summoned to attend the court at
which history will be judged.

BOUCHRA
For me, the table, the four of you,
the photos, were part of an editing room
where history had to be retold and
therefore reactivated.

PHILIPPE
But history is also about 'montage'.
It is also about editing.

BOUCHRA
Exactly. It is the storyboard on which
the 'story' and the 'history' can be
examined. But you said 'trial'. Is it a
'trial' in the sense of 'process' or in the
sense of the courtroom?[1]

PHILIPPE
In the sense of the courtroom, the
courtroom formed by the screen.

BOUCHRA
In a trial an indictment is drafted.
How would you draft it?

PHILIPPE
Let's say that the indictment, or rather the
interrogation, is about this question: as
memory, what is the truth of this memory
in the moment of its reactivation? What
is the truth of 'I remember' in the moment
of me saying 'I remember'? 'I, here, now,
I remember myself': what does it reflect
about history, and the relationship with
the absentees? What is the legitimacy
of this 'I'? What is the legitimacy of this
testimony? Even if I performed words that
were written collectively forty years earlier,
it forced me to ask myself: what is the
legitimacy of those words throughout time?
As Marx said, history does not repeat itself,
it stutters. However, here it's not about
stuttering; it's about resonance.

BOUCHRA
In the film, I would say that history does
not only resonate in the present, it is at
once about resonating and echoing.
But let's go further. On the set, you asked   79
yourself 'What is a witness?', and we see
you listening to these young people, more
than you speak. And when you speak,
you do not speak as a witness but as
a protagonist suddenly anchored in the
present. You are literally an 'apparition'.

PHILIPPE
That's right. I speak as a protagonist of
a specific moment, a moment that was
of yesterday and that suddenly is of today,
both in Athens and in Paris – as well as
elsewhere, because your work will travel.

BOUCHRA
You speak with the words of yesterday,
but in the literal meaning they are of today.

PHILIPPE
And the beauty of this moment is the
youth of those Athenian voices who were
around me.

BOUCHRA

When you came on the set and then went back to Paris, they told me how much they were moved meeting you, but also very disturbed. They said: 'All those weeks during which you translated to us *Les Tiers Idées*, showed us pictures, told us this story again and again, it still seemed abstract to us.'[2] But it was enough for you to appear, for you to become 'true' to them. But 'true' is not the right word. They told me: 'real'. Your story became a reality. It seems to be the reverse shot of your own perception of the filming. You asked yourself about the legitimacy of your presence as a witness. But they asked themselves the very same question from their own position: what is our legitimacy to tell this story?

PHILIPPE

It is not the legitimacy of the witness that is in question here. Perhaps the question is: 'How does the story of which I was a protagonist acquire the legitimacy to resonate with the present time?'

80   BOUCHRA

I absolutely agree with this: how to make history resonate in the present? And, therefore, when history starts to resonate, what images does it produce? What does it say? This visual apparatus was about interrogating the method and the discourse, allowing this resonance. But let me tell you what impressed me the most when you joined the shooting: seeing you watching the monitor on which this short, silent, super 8 film footage is showing, and which we see partially in the film. We see you, in an occupied factory, performing in front of dozens of North African workers on strike. You are performing a cop, wearing denim and with long hair, dancing with Mokhtar, who is wearing a very elegant white suit.

PHILIPPE

In the excerpt we see only a tiny part of the play. For example, we do not see the scene between the two Ministers, the Moroccan Minister of Labour and the French Minister of Labour, discussing the quota of immigrant workers to send to France. In the following scene, we perform the workers arriving in France, wearing cardboard boxes on our heads. But that day, suddenly, we were interrupted by one of the viewers. He started shouting, 'It did not happen like that.' He joined us and showed us how it is to land in France as an immigrant worker. He did not speak. He did not comment. He mimed the scene. And, of course, we watched him doing it. It was completely Brechtian, in terms of distancing effect: a spectator, concerned in the first place with the story we are telling, objects to our version of the story and shows us how to perform that situation and how to stage it.

BOUCHRA

Mokhtar was in the position of this worker who objected. He knew from experience what he meant.

PHILIPPE

But it was still a lesson in theatre for us, a wonderful lesson.

BOUCHRA

During the time that my project lasted, roughly from 2012 to 2017, I always wondered why you had documented your work so little.

PHILIPPE

It was a time when life itself was so strong that we did not feel the need for images, or the need for memory. We never thought we should keep something. Every moment was so intense and unique that we did not need to record them.

BOUCHRA

But isn't it because of that lack of images and traces that you felt summoned to justify yourself as a witness? At that moment, the trace that remains is you, it is your body, your voice, your words, your presence?

PHILIPPE

Of course. For example, I remember writing in 1969 on Censier's walls, 'Let's make sure that what we are doing today never becomes a memory.'[3] But it did not stop me from writing *Les Tiers Idées* with Geneviève ten years after, because we were conscious that the strategies of erasing our struggles were already well underway. So, with Geneviève, we thought that we had to write, that something had to remain of Al Assifa.

ALEXANDRE
Was it also that what you were doing did not belong to you?

PHILIPPE
Absolutely. We did not consider ourselves as authors, with all the authority that the term carries. The only authority we recognised was that of the collective. So when you invited me on the set, I necessarily asked myself, 'What is my right to speak?'

BOUCHRA
I also thought that it was your duty.

PHILIPPE
But it is a very heavy burden. What is the legitimacy of my word in the current context? I am isolated. And that's a question I ask myself every single day: are you up today for what you were up for yesterday? But is there still a space for such question? As long as Al Assifa existed, resistance was still possible because we were contesting the power with our own transmission tools, of which theatre was a part.

BOUCHRA
In retrospect, can we also say that what has changed the balance of power is the issue of alliance? Geneviève and yourself were members of a Palestine committee, Mokhtar too, and he was also one of the founders of the Movement of Arab Workers (MTA). You had a space where you could all meet in the first place.

PHILIPPE
Absolutely. It was a tactical question. We originally belonged to organisations that could appear to be distinct, but that were in fact completely connected.

BOUCHRA
So, regarding the current state of the struggles, I would say that Geneviève and yourself were 'allies'. How would you define the terms of your alliance?

PHILIPPE
What was at stake above all was the struggle. Our position was defined by solidarity and the refusal to be 'collaborators' with the French regime and government. So, we were objective allies. It was also in our interest to help immigrant workers to defend their rights and dignity.

BOUCHRA
Then how, ten years later, did we end up with 'Touche pas à mon pote'?[4]

PHILIPPE
It was all about communication.

BOUCHRA
But beyond communication 'Touche pas à mon pote' was a return to invisibility and an injunction to silence the primary victims. The opposite of what Al Assifa and the MTA were advocating for.

PHILIPPE
Mokhtar and the members of the MTA were not our pals. They were our comrades in struggle. 'Touche pas à mon pote' is the 'Big Bertha' of patronising humanitarianism, used against self-organised politicised groups and political struggle.[5]

ALEXANDRE
In your practice, have you been confronted with workers who were not sympathisers of the struggle for equality between French and immigrant workers?

PHILIPPE
We tried to establish a dialogue, because we had to convince them.

BOUCHRA
So you are saying that as activists, your job was also to convince opponents of your struggle and make them join the fight?

PHILIPPE
Absolutely.

ALEXANDRE
Bouchra, you said that you had missed
having archival material to help your work
on the project?

BOUCHRA
I would rather say that I missed 'pictures'
that could have allowed me to picture for
myself what the performances looked like,
how you looked all together.

PHILIPPE
But there was a lot of improvisation. The
performance was changing all the time,
depending on events – that were immediately
included – because each of us was also
part of political actions and strikes.

BOUCHRA
When you wrote Les Tiers Idées, you
included few excerpts of your plays.
Why did you not include the plays in their
entirety, or at least precise indications?

PHILIPPE
We never considered that others could
perform those plays. That was not the
goal: from the street to the stage, and
from the stage to the street, we were
the same 'protagonists'. But Al Assifa
had a lot of children. Many more groups
came afterwards.

BOUCHRA
You say that it did not make sense to form
a 'repertoire' because you had 'children'.
But filling a family album is supposed
to be for the children. At least you could
have made a booklet.

PHILIPPE
That's right – especially since we also
recorded audiotapes that were distributed
in cafés, which we called Radio Assifa,
a long time before the 'free radios'.
But to us it was a communication tool
that participated directly in the solidarity
that welded our group. It was not about
theatre for the sake of theatre.

ALEXANDRE
There was no desire to do theatre?

PHILIPPE
It did not arise like that after May '68.
If you look at 1789 or 1793, there is a
gigantic theatrical explosion among
the revolutionary people. It came with
the birth of the revolutionary citizen.
It is the immediacy of the theatre that
accompanies historical upheaval.

BOUCHRA
In 1789 or 1793, or during the Commune,
there was no cinema. But cinema played
a major role in the movement of '68 and
its aftermath.

PHILIPPE
That's right. The cinema was very, very
important. '68 was an eruption of creativity
that aimed to declare the death sentence
of bourgeois art.'68 and the few years
that followed can be understood as an
insurrection that invented a creative life
that did not need to be documented. For
example, the archives of '68 are many,
but when '68 is depicted, we always
see the same images. The images that
were dedicated to recording what was
happening at that time could not capture
what happened. What image could pretend
not to reduce the scope of what happened?
And, mostly because our question was
fully militant: how can our artistic approach
help to blow on the embers and keep them
burning? It was not meant to remain as an
artistic experiment. It was our contribution
to the struggle. It is just my opinion, but
what was dominant at the time was: one
day, we'll have to remember, but what
should be remembered? That was the
idea behind Les Tiers Idées: what do
we remember?

BOUCHRA
But if you look at the films of members of
the Medvedkin Group, for example, it was
about workers on strike who made films
to document the struggle and share it with
the public, and some of these films were
also amazing pieces of art.[6]

PHILIPPE

Of course, it was a cinema that was rooted in the struggle, and that was filled with the creativity of the struggle itself.

BOUCHRA

In the case of the Medvedkin Group, professional filmmakers considered that it was the workers themselves who had to represent their struggle, so these filmmakers put themselves at the service of these workers by teaching them how to use filming and editing and then letting them make their own films. It has become a method. And it also showed that it was possible to document the struggle just as it was happening. So the question was not to produce archives. Why did you not document the struggle as part of the struggle?

PHILIPPE

It is true that we rested on a glorious body. Al Assifa toured from 1973 to 1977. We went performing every weekend in different regions of France, in Belgium, Switzerland. That makes 120 weekends, not counting the performances during the week because a strike had broken out at such and such a place. It must represent 300 performances in four years. Of course, a lot of pictures were taken, and certainly some movies were shot. There must be hundreds of documents, but we did not care about who photographed or filmed or about where these documents might be.

BOUCHRA

Yet you knew that the best way to erase the memory of struggles is to erase any traces, in order to erase them from the collective memory.

PHILIPPE

Of course. But we were protagonists in a struggle, not the witnesses. For us the act of resistance was indelible from the moment it took place. For me, the question and concern about trace begins to arise from 1985.

BOUCHRA

Why 1985?

PHILIPPE

Because I could have a camera, and also because the isolation became bigger. I told myself that if I do not start gathering traces, everything would disappear in a big chasm. To use the metaphor of Abdellatif Laabi, I thought it was time to take a sewing needle and start digging between the stones.[7]

BOUCHRA

Don't you think that it was a bit late?

PHILIPPE

I understand very well that I can be challenged on the issue of documenting our struggle. But let me quote you René Char: *when the resistance arrived, I got involved, and I decided to take some notes to write poems for after the war, but I would not write poems as long as the war lasted.*

BOUCHRA

Then I can answer you with the Pasolini's poem quoted in the film: *I came to the world at the time of the Analogic. I worked in that field, as apprentice. Then there was the Resistance and I fought with the weapons of poetry. I restored logic and was a civil poet.*

PHILIPPE

Char did not say that he would not write more poems; he said that he would write them after the war. But as long as he was in the Resistance, he wouldn't write poems with a rifle in his hands.

BOUCHRA

I agree. Pasolini was not in the Resistance. It is his brother Guido who joined the Resistance, and who was killed. Pasolini wrote poems of the glory of the Resistance and decided to embody the figure of the civil poet who speaks for the absentees and the silenced ones. In a way, your collective position was also the one of the civil poet as defined by Pasolini.

83

PHILIPPE

Racism and all enslavement are based on dehumanisation. For one who refuses this dehumanisation, the question is: how do I recover my humanity? And this is not an aesthetic question, it is a question that arises in the moment of struggle.

BOUCHRA

And you thought that the stage was a site for struggle, for retrieving humanity?

PHILIPPE

For us, performance was the immediate tool by which the one deprived of the right to self-representation and who does not have the right to speech can suddenly arise. What matters is this emergence of the invisible one, which is already a gesture of pure theatricality: the one who has been dehumanised by the ones in power begins to assert his existence and his identity. By portraying himself in front of an audience, he creates an image that resists silence. For example, when you start to fight back, you also start to challenge the image that the power forces you to accept, which can be summarised as: 'The job I'm giving you makes you exist as a human being and defines your identity.' From the moment you rise in rebellion, you destroy the identification of yourself as defined by capitalism and society.

Rebelling is the break with this identification. From that moment, the question becomes: 'How am I going to represent myself for myself? And, therefore, what tools, what means, will I use to produce that self-representation?' Of course, power understands it as a gesture of destruction, although I do not break anything – I am just producing my own image in contrast to the one imposed on me and which I know is alienating me. As a form of resistance, I will claim and produce the image of my radical otherness, against the exploiters.

BOUCHRA

But your audience was not made of the exploiters, but of the exploited

PHILIPPE

Yes, but these exploited ones, what did they see on the stage? They saw a space of affirmation and pride of this otherness against the values of the exploiters. The stage and the performance were the site from where a protest could be elaborated: 'You exploiters, you are the agents of our acculturation. By presenting myself on stage, I show you that I am fighting against you, with what I am, a radical alien to you, contesting the values that you aim to impose on us.'

BOUCHRA

I understand. However, your audience had a culture. When they laugh at the scenes showing confrontation between exploiters and the exploited, they laugh with their culture. And it is with their culture that their laugh ridiculed the exploiters.

PHILIPPE

Absolutely. At that moment, their laughter is cultural in the sense that they laugh with their own cultures, against the culture of the exploiters.

BOUCHRA

So, in a sense, Al Assifa performed for an audience, in the name of a culture that was despised and silenced.

PHILIPPE

Absolutely. Often the predicate of 'culture' is defined from the perspective of the exploiters perpetuating their blackmail: 'If you want to work, you have to accept our "culture", so put aside yours, and shut up.' So what Al Assifa was showing on stage was, 'I no longer accept this blackmail, because I exist independently of this dilution of myself and of my culture imposed by the employers and the exploiters.'

BOUCHRA

What you are describing is also a form of resistance to a colonial continuum. For example, these men we see laughing in the short super 8 excerpt, fifteen years before, they were colonised.

The acculturation attempt you describe already existed in the colonial process.

PHILIPPE
Absolutely. What we are talking about here is the political position of Al Assifa: 'We are immigrant workers and we perform to testify to our condition and fight for our rights. We impose ourselves on your territory to challenge the representations you make of us and that you aim to impose on us. 'Since you tell us that we are workers who are not entitled to speak, we come to tell you that we have a culture, that we can speak for ourselves, and that not only do we have a culture but that we can produce our own culture.' Nevertheless, in that context, even the progressive forces, including the media, did not accept it, because they began to say: 'As long as you were narrating your suffering as migrant workers, we could stand in solidarity, but now that you pretend to produce theatrical forms, we can't support you anymore. We are the ones deciding what is art and what is not.'

BOUCHRA
You raise a critical point. What you are saying is that as long as Al Assifa presented itself as a militant group, you aroused sympathy among the intelligentsia. But from the moment you claim to be producing theatrical forms, the situation changed.

PHILIPPE
Absolutely. Progressives have begun to say: 'Know your place. We are the ones with the legitimacy to judge. We want to support you in the name of human rights, but do not start to claim to be creative. Among them were activists, intellectuals, journalists, theatre people. But for us, producing theatrical forms was not to affirm human rights, it was to affirm "the rights of the being".'

BOUCHRA
So, at first, the judges stand on the same side as you and then they turn their backs on you because you started claiming

that you also produce theatrical forms. But who are those judges?

PHILIPPE
Let me rather tell you who continued to support us: Michel Foucault, his partner Daniel Defert, Claude Mauriac, Sartre, Deleuze. They remained consistent and supportive, as well as a small crowd of young activists.

BOUCHRA
So how would you define those who fell on you?

PHILIPPE
They were intellectuals, 'bourgeois de l'érudition' (the bourgeois of erudition). They said: 'As long as you remain activists, your performances are great. Bravo, we support you. But art is serious, and it's our business, not yours.'

ALEXANDRE
And the theatre people, how did they react?

PHILIPPE
Some supported us and took our work seriously. For example, Alain Cuny came to see us and told us: 'I'm not here only to support your cause, but because you're teaching me something about theatre too.'[8] There were many others – like the 'Black Oak Theatre' who invited us to Avignon to perform, where the audience paid for their tickets. On the same day, we were also in a public space, on the Palais des Papes Place, where 250 North African workers gathered to see us performing for free. It was the same play, but we performed it differently, because in this configuration we were in the traditional situation in Morocco of 'Al-Halqa': the storyteller surrounded by an audience in a public space, on a square.[9]

BOUCHRA
But when you played on a real stage it was also a 'Halqa'.

PHILIPPE

Absolutely. The storyteller's position was fundamental. As a Frenchman and a member of Al Assifa, the storyteller's function in Morocco was a huge discovery. I had the impression of discovering Brecht a long time before Brecht had existed. The interpellations between the storyteller and the audience were not the winks of the actor to the public, as in western theatre. The interpellation in the *Halqa*'s tradition was a real and equal interaction. The storyteller has no word of authority: he is the bearer of a collective and historical speech that can be contested at the moment of its public performance.

BOUCHRA

And sometimes you also performed for an audience made of French viewers. How did you feel performing for that audience?

PHILIPPE

We had to convince, and in such a situation we always made a point of performing with a great sense of authority.

BOUCHRA

Convincing the bourgeoisie when one leads an anti-racist struggle that crosses over with the class struggle – wasn't that a contradiction?

PHILIPPE

Yes, but we needed to make alliances. We were aware that we were on their field. But our goal was also to take possession of that field and to confront them.

BOUCHRA

So you considered that performing in a real theatre was also the right place to conduct the struggle?

PHILIPPE

Absolutely. But it was very hard. And yet it also allowed us to evaluate the stakes of the fight. We could not just stick to factories and workers' shelters. We had to confront and oppose those French viewers on their own field, in order to raise awareness among them – even if it was just in a few.

BOUCHRA

However, your 'natural' audience was the North African workers. And the question of solidarity and internationalism at the time was much more significant than it is today.

PHILIPPE

Absolutely. This is what brought us closer to Arab workers and students: Palestine, the anti-colonial struggles and the struggle against imperialism. And what was very clear to us too was that the Palestinian struggle was revolutionary, because it was a laboratory of emancipation.

BOUCHRA

So the question of emancipation in the Palestinian revolution echoed the anti-racist struggle in France as led by Arab workers and students.

PHILIPPE

Absolutely. This struggle resonated with the anti-colonial struggles elsewhere – in the same way that it continued the anti-colonial struggle led by the North African peoples against French colonialism twenty years earlier.

BOUCHRA

And these workers and students that settled after independence were also not strangers to the struggles in their home countries against authoritarian regimes. What was the relationship between Al Assifa and the MTA? For the MTA, the aesthetic modalities of the fight were not a priority, right?

PHILIPPE

Al Assifa was happening inside the struggles. There was indeed a debate within the MTA, but I won't call it a break. Al Assifa claimed, 'We seize the theatre, because it has immediate effect: we speak for ourselves and we make ourselves heard.' It was right. There's no doubt that the movement that was born jointly from the MTA and Al Assifa did not see in the same way that culture was a space for struggle. But they understood it later.

ALEXANDRE
ALEXANDRE
In your plays, you also denounced the pitfall
of victimisation.

PHILIPPE
That's why we adopted specific theatrical
strategies. For example, in Ça travaille,
ça travaille there is a scene of bludgeoning,
which arrives abruptly, in absolute silence.[10]
We see the bludgeoning of a young Arab
worker by a French cop. This unexpected
appearance and silence were very powerful.
You could really see this confrontation.
The worker turns the other cheek as
a challenge: 'I know you want to kill me,
but are you capable of doing it?'

Offering the other cheek is not a gesture
of surrender, but of defiance, stating,
'Look at me: I am a human being, so are
you still capable of killing a human being?
By showing that, there is the affirmation
of the full dignity of humanity in the face
of the cop's inhumanity.

BOUCHRA
This is my last question. You knew
Al-Halqa's tradition and its performance
strategies. You also knew Brecht. How
did you articulate the relationship between
these two forms of performance that
involve both distancing and interaction
with the audience?

PHILIPPE
Brecht was not central. Our question was
how to politicise our roles and functions.
Brecht, like most people who theorise,
started from the real and the concrete.
And a real intelligence can only be grateful
to the rebels. Can we say that if Brecht
had not existed, our actions would have
been different? Of course, they would
have been different.

BOUCHRA
We spoke of many different things at once.
Shall we go back to our initial question?
What do we do with history and memory?
Who is entitled to carry the burden of its
transmission?

PHILIPPE
The important thing is not to remember,
but to reflect on what we can remember.
Or in other words: it is not the witness
or the testimony that matters, but to
reflect on the function of the witness
and on that of the testimony.

1

In French, 'procès' refers both to the trial and to the 'process'

2

Les Tiers Idées, by Geneviève Clancy and Philippe Tancelin, Hachette, 1977, (p. 267). The title was suggested by Mohamed 'Mokhtar' Bachiri.

3

Censier is the site of Université de la Sorbonne Nouvelle.

4

Literally 'Hands off my pal'. It was the motto of 'SOS Racisme', an NGO created and instrumentalised by the French Socialist Party to destroy the autonomous anti-racist movement that was rising in France after the massive success of the self-organised March for Equality and Against Racism (from October to December 1983).

5

Big Bertha is the name of a type of super-heavy siege artillery developed by the armaments manufacturer Krupp in Germany and used in World Wars I and II. Besides its official designation, the name 'Big Bertha' subsequently came to be applied generically by the Allies to any very large German gun.

6

In 1967, responding to an invitation by workers at the Rhodiaceta textile factory in Besançon, Chris Marker, joined by Jean-Luc Godard, trained workers to do filmmaking and editing in order to support their struggle. The first two films – À bientôt, j'espère (1968), and Classe de Lutte (1969) – were co-directed by Marker and the workers, who then started making their own films. In 1968, a second group was initiated by filmmaker Bruno Muel at the Peugeot factory in Sochaux. The groups were named after the collectivist Soviet filmmaker Aleksandr Medvedkin and his 'cine-train'.

7

A Moroccan poet, born in 1942 in Fes, Morocco, Laabi is one of the most important and celebrated poets from North Africa and the Middle East. He founded the legendary avant-garde art and cultural magazine Souffles (1966–1972). He was also the co-founder of Ila Ala Amane, a Moroccan underground radical leftist movement. For his writings and political opinions, Laabi was arrested in 1972 and tortured. In 1973 he was sentenced to ten years in prison, which he spent mostly in the infamous Kenitra prison. He was eventually released in 1980 after a massive international campaign. He currently lives between Créteil (suburb of Paris) and Rabat.

8

Alain Cuny (1908–1994): French actor in theatre and cinema, mostly known for his performances in the films of Marcel Carné, Louis Malle, Federico Fellini, Buñuel, and Godard, among many others. He also performed in many plays staged by legendary French theatre director Jean Vilar, founder of the Festival d'Avignon and the TNP (People's National Theatre). Cuny is among the signatories of the 'Manifeste des 121' published on 6 September 1960, claiming the right of insubordination in the Algerian war and stating that the cause of the Algerians was the cause of all free men.

9

Al-Halqa is a public gathering in the form of a circle around a performer or a number of performers (hlayqi/hlayqia) in a public space, be it a marketplace, a medina gate, or a newly devised downtown square. It is a space of popular culture that is open to all people from different walks of life. Al-Halqa hovers between high culture and low mass culture, sacred and profane, literacy and orality. Its repertoire combines fantastic, mythical, and historical narratives from A Thousand and One Nights and Sirat bani hilal, as well as stories from the Quran and the Sunna of the prophet Mohammed. The form of the halqa also varies from storytelling to acrobatic acting and dancing. The most ancient form of public performance in Morocco (probably from the ninth century), today it is disappearing. See 'Crossing Borders, Al-Halqa Performance in Morocco from the Open Space to the Theatre Building', by Khalid Amine, The Drama Review, Vol. 45, issue 2, (pp. 55–69), MIT Press, 2006. Khalili has often addressed the importance of this tradition in her work.

10

Ça travaille, ça travaille, et ça ferme sa gueule (Work, Work, and Shut your Mouth): Al Assifa's first play.

Not nostalgia
and patriotism

Mokhtar created
for imn

first free radio

ants

RASSEMBLEMENT   CULTU

DIMANCHE 2.

AVEC LA TROUPE DE

THÉATRE
EL
ALAKA
DES TRAVAILLEURS
ARABES D'AIX

TROUPE
FOLKLORIQUE
DES
TRAVAILLEURS
ARABES
DE CLERMONT.FD

DES
TRAVAILLEURS
MAROCAINS
DE CHAUSSON
ET
"GENERAL
MOTORS"

يلعمال

...L DES TRAVAILLEURS ARABES

FÉVRIER 14ʰ

DES FEMMES ARABES
DE MARSEILLE
QUI JOUENT UNE PIÈCE
SUR
LES CONDITIONS
DE TRAVAIL
DES FEMMES DE MÉNAGE
ARABES

DES
MILITANTS
DU
M.T.A
DE
-PARIS -AIX- MARSEILLE-
-TOULOUSE -

MAISON
DU
PEUPLE

ΤΑΓΜΑ
2015

The Tempest Society: Towards a Politics and Poetics of Emancipation

Pothiti Hantzaroula

In the midst of a financial and refugee crisis, a major cultural event took place in Athens. In the context of documenta 14, Bouchra Khalili's *The Tempest Society* is directly related to the Greek financial crisis and to the assault on democracy with which it was met by established European and global power.[1] Its focus on Greece aims at producing alternative conceptions of civic community, belonging, and resistance. Greece is viewed as a space in which transnational processes overlap with concern for the global economic crisis or with the migratory moves of the last decade. It is also the place in which significant political mobilisation and practices which challenged power structures emerged. During the last decade, an extensive network of grass-roots initiatives of solidarity outside the auspices and mediation of the state and other institutions developed.

The Tempest Society, though related to the Greek dual crisis, economic and migratory, cannot be confined solely to Greece as each locality brings forward elements of global connections, not because of the existence of *The Family of Man*, but due to inequalities that have their origin in colonial domination or to economic power relations enforced by the neoliberal establishment.[2] Locality can also serve as a platform for the civic, where potential collectives emerge from subjective accounts of embodied geographies which open up possibilities for acts of resistance to come into existence.

Khalili's work lacks a master historical narrative. As *The Opposite of Voice-Over*,[3] it stands against a system of information operating on the basis of selecting who is capable of deciphering information and teaching us that not just anyone is capable of seeing and speaking.[4] It aims at surpassing the spectator/actor divide by promoting the viewers' own connections and experiences, and by bringing their interpretations to the fore. Forgotten connections could be recalled, from the ancient Greek drama to the performing art of *halqa* in Morocco;[5] visions could be revitalised, in which the struggle for citizenship rights is connected to artistic emancipation. Such an approach serves not only the transgression of all enclosures of ethnic identity but also the process of demystification.[6] By placing *The Tempest Society* in the context of the Greek dual crises, unlearning also takes place in Khalili's project as a process devoted to intellectual emancipation based on the equality of thinkers. This means also addressing the spectator as an actor who composes her own poem by using the elements of poetry she has before her.[7]

GREEK ECONOMIC CRISIS

The crisis of European capitalism, which created the lowest investment in history and affected the Greek economy, was treated in the case of Greece as an isolated event and not as part of a global crisis. The country was called to converge to Balkan and Latin American wage levels.[8]

The system of economic surveillance and political regulation and the austerity measures introduced within the framework of Memoranda signed with the Troika – the European Union, European Central Bank and International Monetary Fund

(EU, ECB and IMF) – promoted the deregulation and increased flexibilisation of the labour market, the reduction of minimum wages and salaries, and the abandonment of collective bargaining.

Public discourse at a national and international level presented the Greek economic crisis as the country's individual problem, related to the high standard of living that the Greek population supposedly enjoyed and for which Greek workers had to be penalised. Moreover, Greek workers had been presented as working less than other Europeans and receiving too much in social protection. But as scholars such as Papatheodorou, Sakellaropoulos and Yeros have shown, these assumptions lack any empirical plausibility: the average hours that Greeks work per week in their main jobs are the highest among all the EU-27 countries, a finding which undermines the view of Greek profligacy.[9] And compared to the Europeans, despite their working more hours, Greeks also have one of the highest rates of poverty.[10] The minimum net monthly wage for full-time employment among young employees is lower than the country's poverty line for a single person in 2010.[11] Considering the above picture, unemployment should not be considered as the sole cause of poverty due to the economic crisis.

Although it was argued that Greeks enjoyed high standards of living before the crisis compared to other Europeans, estimates on poverty rates in the EU show that 38.2% of the Greek population have a low standard of living comparable to that of the 13.3% poorest Danes and that of the 10.05% poorest Dutch. During the pre-crisis period the relative poverty risk in Greece was also considerably higher than the corresponding average figure for EU-15 and EU-27. The average poverty rate in Greece for the period 1995–2012 was the highest among all EU-15 countries, and during the same period, poverty risk in Greece was 20.07%. To speak of further popular perceptions, social spending

in Greece was considered particularly generous and to have contributed to the huge public debt. However, for most of the pre-crisis period, social expenditure in Greece as a percentage of GDP has been significantly lower than corresponding figures across the EU-15 and EU-27.[12]

The economic and neo-liberal austerity measures implemented in Greece during the economic crisis had devastating effects on the system of social welfare and on the mechanisms of social protection. The pre-existing inadequacies of the social protection system further weakened and people sank even deeper into poverty than they had in the previous decades. The Greek social protection system – historically characterised by fragmentation and uncoordinated provision, with families playing a crucial role in social care[13] – became even more inadequate in its capacity to address social risks such as unemployment, inequality and poverty.[14]

Poverty severely affected new, wider strata of society and simultaneously hit with greater vehemence the population already living below the poverty line. Although official data has been used both by government and media to propagate a view of poverty reduction over the last couple of years, Papatheodorou and Dafermos have shown, by using the same poverty threshold of a particular base year, that the percentage of the population living below the poverty line increased from 18.9% in 2008 to 40% in 2016. Furthermore, poverty risk increased dramatically between 2010 and 2011, and the poor became poorer in an overlapping time period: the poverty gap enlarged significantly from 23.4% in 2008 to 29.9% in 2011. In terms of deprivation, Greece is the most deprived among European countries, with a chasm setting it remarkably far from the countries that hold the second and third places. When the austerity measures were introduced, in just one year the proportion of the population living below the poverty line increased by eleven percentage units.[15]

The impact of the economic crisis on poverty and on the deterioration of the living standards of the most vulnerable population groups has not led to a change of the dominant paradigm for organising and administering modern capitalist economies. On the contrary, as Christos Papatheodorou argues, 'the recent economic crisis has served as an alibi for further strengthening the neo-liberal policies for fiscal discipline, reduction of public spending and labour market deregulation.'[16]

Since it has been demonised as a contributor to the burgeoning public debt, social welfare during the crisis has not increased. Yet social expenditure has been significantly lower than the average corresponding figures for the EU. Elderly people with no rights to social insurance, immigrants, the long-term unemployed (particularly unemployed women), young people without qualifications and/or work experience, as well as those employed in an underground economy face a heightened risk of poverty as hardly any social protection exists for them.[17]

The crisis has become a ruling mechanism by which political and economic decisions are legitimised: a mode of governance that aims at depriving citizens of any possibility of making a decision of their own. New narratives were invented and new governing mechanisms were improvised to bend the rise of grassroots initiatives that challenged the hegemonic socio-economic policies. In the discourse of crisis by the governing elite, uncertainty was identified as its core feature. Yiannis Kallianos argues that in the restructuring of the state under neo-liberal government, uncertainty becomes a governing technology that defines 'the symbolic universe' of the crisis. Uncertainty as an apparatus of control produces a new social contract in which the subject is 'productive' in conditions of radical uncertainty.[18]

Greece shifted in the nineteen-eighties from a country of emigration to a migrant-receiving country. Although migration to Greece started in the 1970s, Greece became an immigrant country in the 1980s, when a growing number of male migrants from Third World countries were employed in the manufacturing sector and a growing number of female migrants were employed in the service sector. Citizenship rights were curtailed due to the prohibitions migrants faced in terms of visa extensions, job mobility, work conditions, and welfare rights.[19]

In the 1990s a new wave of migration from the Balkans and Eastern Europe to Greece began. Migrant workers started their journey from their homelands into Greece with the collapse of governments, welfare systems, traditional work regulations, and mobility opportunities based on education and work expectations.[20] Neo-liberal economic restructuring, the dismantling of the welfare state, and migration policies created the international division of reproductive labour according to which poor migrant workers provide care for families in rich countries with higher incomes.[21]

As Iordanis Psimmenos argues, the exploration of the relationship between economic recession and workers' lives has to be placed in the context of the historic transformation of migrant workers' social and civic status in Europe and Greece. Migrant labour is characterised by new forms of slavery and bondage based on emotional relationships between employer and employee, non-recognition of social rights, and by a working culture that abandons workers in a 'black' economy. One has also to take into account their market value, work prospects, and social status related to broad historical and social processes and connected to their ethnicity and gender.[22] Migrants occupy the lowest strata of the labour market (construction workers, agricultural

98

workers, domestic workers) or enter unregulated, or sexual services labour markets (for example, prostitution). Studies have shown migrant workers are marginalised in terms of access to welfare, social security and social rights.

The current policy of labour market deregulation was preceded by a massive violation of migrant labour rights. Konstantina Kouneva, now a Member of the European Parliament elected as a candidate of SYRIZA and former Secretary of the Panattic Union of Cleaners and Domestic Staff (PEKOP) was the victim of an acid attack in December 2008. Sulphuric acid was thrown on her, forcing her to swallow it, in an attempt to silence her for her union activity and to go as far as to kill her. Kouneva, who previously worked as a cleaner in Athens and at the Piraeus Electric Railway Company under a subcontracting system, fought for the labour rights of cleaners whose contracts were infringed. A massive solidarity movement followed the attack, and her message on 1 May 2014 was addressed to domestic cleaners: 'Today let your mops down and say: Look at us! We have flesh, bones and a voice.' (Five hundred cleaning workers were protesting after they were sacked by the Ministry of Finance for the benefit of a private cleaning corporation.)[23]

In the last two decades, the migrant populations that enter Greek territory originate from Asia and Africa and, without papers, they live hidden lives in the grey zone of bureaucracy. During the refugee crisis in 2015, Lesvos was the main gateway to Europe for people travelling from the Middle East and Africa. According to the United Nations High Commissioner for Refugees (UNHCR), 500,018 people arrived on the island, with this number representing the fortunate ones who survived the crossing of the Aegean Sea in rubber dinghies.[24] Those who crossed the border received an administrative order dictating that those who were classified as Syrians, Somalis or of a non-deportable nationality should leave the country voluntarily within a period of six months, while those of other nationalities were given one month to go.[25] In October 2015, the Moria hotspot was inaugurated, where all bordering bureaucratic procedures take place. After March 2016 and with the 'EU-Turkey Deal', the Moria camp entered a new phase in the EU border regime. Border-crossers who arrived in Lesvos after the signing of the 'EU-Turkey Deal' would remain for twenty-eight days under administrative detention in the Moria camp and for an indefinite period beyond that on the island.[26] The legal category of the asylum seeker was offered as an option to this population. Evthymios Papataxiarchis argues that although this legal category existed, its transformation into an identity entailed the insertion of the asylum seeker into a total humanitarian system constituting a form of governance – with its own economic base and superstructure, articulated through a legal discourse on rights, and a patriotism of solidarity.[27] According to Papataxiarchis, this new phase in the management of the refugee crisis, which resulted in the emergence of the 'humanitarian city', would be capable of paving the way to the creation of a new form of symbiosis between the refugee and local population.[28]

THE POLITICS OF AESTHETICS

In the last years, there has been a prevalence of art that is sensitive to questions raised by history and anthropology, concerning issues of immigration or economic crisis and deprivation, both in European and non-European countries. This has led to a transgression of disciplinary boundaries and to an engagement of various actors. Experience, and more precisely the experience of the other, has been put at the centre of artistic inquiry as accompanying concerns around identity. The question of experience is what documenta 14 'Learning from Athens' points to, as a call to learn from the Greek experience of the economic crisis.

Intellectual emancipation is the aim, with the means proposed through a transformation of the roles of creator and spectator.

In 1996, Hal Foster analysed the impact of anthropology in contemporary art through two important categories, of identity and identification. According to Foster, the economic other – i.e., the proletariat in avant-garde art – is substituted by the cultural other in contemporary art, by the artist taking an ethnographic, othering position.[29] At least two problems arise here, following Foster's argument. Political truth is located in the other or in the outside, but, first, the outside is not other and, second, the location of politics in the outside and in the other can distract from a politics of the here and now.

Khalili's historical and anthropological perspectives need to be differentiated from artistic fascination with ethnography, as they stem from a different position, of reactivating the tradition of 'civic poetry'. Her location of political truth is not in the outside but in the 'inside other' and more precisely in such 'inside others' as the Greek as European inside-other, the economic other (in the EU Greeks facing the threat of being ousted from the Union due to their supposedly superfluous spending), and the cultural other (the migrant in Greece). The singular voice speaking in her work activates mnemonic traces of the inside-others' subjection in power structures as well as new collective subjectivities and resistant formations.

In her 2002 publication *One Place after Another*, Miwon Kwon critiques the notion of 'community' in artistic work.[30] Drawing on Jean-Luc Nancy's reconceptualisation of community as being-in-common, she argues that '[o]nly a community that questions its own legitimacy is legitimate,'[31] and suggests community be viewed not as a product of work or projected labour but as an *un-working* and collective artistic praxis as an un-siting of community.[32]

In Khalili's work, community neither functions as a referential social entity nor does it represent a coherent collective subject. Taking inspiration from Al Assifa (translated as 'the Tempest') theatre group, Khalili does not perceive of community as an expression of an identity immanent to itself. In Khalili's *The Tempest Society*, but also in Al Assifa's work, community is formed in the artistic performance as process: of interaction, identification, misidentification, and disidentification among the subjects – actors, artists, spectators – involved. This is a community formed by those who did not identify with a community. *The Tempest Society* is in this respect a palimpsest of identifications in which the enactment of speech leads to new constellations of transnational civic belonging and resistance.

The film endorses a participatory model of art practice in order to create an alternative narrative about the past, an 'alternative historiography' written by the actors who compose a family album of ancestors they have chosen.[33] The family album is where the film starts, engaging local concerns and people, yet the ancestors chosen are neither geographic nor temporal locals: they come from a collective established in 1972 in Paris by a North African worker who migrated to France from Morocco in 1969, and two French students. The 1972 Tempest collective paid tribute to Al Assifa, a Palestinian resistance organisation, and Khalili's Tempest Society as a palimpsest evokes a past, the elements of which are still with us, weaving unexpected connections. The participatory model of art practice is used as method for the film's production and by the actors' conception of their roles. As Philippe Tancelin, a member of the Al Assifa collective, states, 'we are not playing theatre but narrate the fight for the rights of migrant workers in France.' The stage on which the collective plays is that of the civic poet (in Pasolini's terms) who fights with poetry as a weapon.[34]

Khalili's project is permeated by a political opening to the other, with the other not representing the figure of a reified victim or beneficiary. The subjects speak their own language, which embodies the social, political and psychological baggage of their background. Khalili's voice merges with that of the protagonists constituting the 'indirect free subjectivity' that establishes in cinema the language of poetry.[35] The promise of solidarity and collectivity is not premised upon exclusion, ban and separation. As Leela Gandhi writes, the political opening to the other is more about 'naming a relation, or putting forth relationality [...] rendering politics into a performance of strange alliance, unlikely kinships, and impossible identification.'[36] By 'telling the story', as the actors proclaim, memory becomes a political tool and a form of consciousness that creates novel collectivities and networks of solidarity, which are not based on national or family commemorations, patriotism or identity politics but on assembling traces and images of the past with present emancipatory aims. These new constellations produce political developments concerning rights as well as new forms of political action. The material from which civic identity is woven – based on solidarity, freedom, and equality – produces a poetic enunciation, a constant 'now' that synchronises past, present and future as it transmits state violence and exclusion.[37] Subjects emerge not as passive victims of processes of globalisation and power but as artists producing novel ideas and practices. Malek Lasrae created a theatrical play based on the stories of a number of Syrian children he worked with, as part of 'a politics of a voice speaking for itself, a politics of life that opens a door into the light in the middle of the darkness caused by the war'. Theatre was conceived in this work as 'a space of peace' and as a space respecting the participants' words.

A critical debate unfolds around the film's engagement with contemporary socio-economic issues by giving voice to subjects situated at the margins of society or national identity. Their experiences encompass the history of migration, colonialism, suppression and rebellion. Positioned in a circle that conjures the ancient theatre, the actors perform a similar act of civic practice discussing questions of citizenship, equality and being-in-common. 'When does one stop being a foreigner?' asks Elias Tzogonas, who has lived in Athens for twenty-six years and has to renew his residence permit. The same question applies to the experience of Katerina Barbojias, who has no citizenship rights although she was born in Athens in 1988 and possesses only a birth certificate as proof of identity. In a poetic manner, Elias Tzogonas, interpellated as a 'Greek boy' by his compatriots and as 'Black' by Athenians, has improvised his own calendar, where months are described sensorially, in accordance with Greek attitudes towards him and the way these attitudes are felt:

'I like Athens in August a lot, because I don't hear any swear words. It's the month I can forget that I am Black. I count the time on my skin. [...] In September the swear words return as everybody returns to work, to jammed streets, and to stress. October is the peak. [...] Easter is the sweetest period.'

The film creates a genealogy of struggles for the rights of the people, struggles that became catalysts for the development of new coalitions and alliances. Among these is the hunger strike in January 2011 of 300 migrant workers in Athens and Thessaloniki who left Crete and occupied the Law School of Athens – a politically symbolic place where the student struggle against dictatorship began in 1973 – the conditions of possibility of which were dependent on the existence of a solidarity movement interacting with immigrants. The fight for migrant rights, as recounted by Ghani, founding member of the Association of the Arab Maghreb in Crete, was a struggle for true citizenship which initiated a disruption of the settled state of recognised differences. In the era of crisis, which for Kostas Douzinas is an identity crisis, 'what was invisible, unspoken and unspeakable (under the pre-existing rules) came to the fore.'[38]

The collective actions that took place publicly in Athens created a renegotiation of identities and a new, non-state-defined culture of politics and understanding of the public sphere. Criticism of institutional power and parliamentary democracy became a new feature of the public square movement. The continuous public protests since the introduction of austerity measures culminating in October 2011 challenged the myth of a homogeneous community. As Kallianos argues, reinforcing the argument of Stavros Stavridis, during the crisis new communities were formed as communities in movement, and the singular truth of the sovereign gave way to a multitude of truths.

The process of political radicalisation that took place in the Greek public sphere has its origins in the events of December 2008. As Kallianos points out, the revolt of December 2008 after the murder of Alexandros Grigoropulos, a fifteen-year-old pupil, by police in Athens, while drawing from previous social struggles initiated not only a new understanding of everyday life but an attack on the homogeneous category of 'the people'. December 2008 'unleashed a collective political force whose collective practice and spatial reach had never been seen in Greek territory until then.' Mourning, in Kallianos's view, became 'a public matter in political terms.'

Spatial practices of disorder – repeated mass gatherings and unrest – created groundbreaking experiences of the city and a new public memory, which was inclusive insofar as it gave voice to subjectivities that had previously been excluded. Kallianos has elaborated on such practices in a number of articles from 2013 and 2014, arguing that, in the context of crisis, engagement with the

102

public space challenged official navigation structures connected with official memory and the conceptualisation of public spaces as commercial, under surveillance, controlled and clearly demarcated. Demonstrations, riots, and spontaneous marching are interconnected practices of positioning and acting spatially in public. The paths made during the 2008 assemblies and demonstrations created a new geography that transgressed the monopolisation of public space by the state and the imposition of its interpretation of historical events.[39] The state's domination of public space through the inscription of an official public memory is connected not only with the wielding of control over the past but also with the stakes of the present: the uses of the past play a crucial role in the legitimisation of political decisions. Yet, routes and paths have also incorporated a memory of political unrest, as a memory of political struggle is embodied in certain public spaces.[40] Certain public spaces, streets and squares constitute a spatial representation of events that forged radical politics, such as the November 1944 battles after the German occupation between the National Liberation Front and the right wing co-operation with British allies, or the November 1973 uprising of students in the Polytechnic School against the dictatorial regime. Thus, the use of the same paths and squares not only forges new practices with political meaning but also inscribes new meanings in historically significant space, creating new genealogies.

THE POETICS OF POLITICS

Rancière writes about a politics of aesthetics which pertains to the ability of anybody to recover control of their own destiny. *The Tempest Society* subscribed, as we have seen, to such a politics of emancipation. In the film's poetics of politics, the immobility of the actors and the fixed camera lift the established dichotomy between discourse and action, actor and spectator, and invite the viewer to engage and reflect actively.

The spectator becomes a thinker, participant in an action that transforms the distribution of positions through processes of observation, interpretation and comparison.

Emancipation is not only intellectual, but also affective. As an affect theorist, Teresa Brennan is interested in the ways in which new ethics of relationality are enabled by affect as it breaks down the subject/object divide.[41] Affect is the body's response to stimuli at a precognitive and prelinguistic level but it nevertheless involves a kind of judgment enacted at the level of the body. Affect requires a view of the body as radically open to the world, existing in a continuum in which the terms 'subject' and 'object' make no sense. This also means ceasing to privilege vision over the other senses, since vision is what constructs the seeing person as subject and the person seen as object. Affect, as Brennan argues, means to be affected by and to affect; it shows that 'we are not self-contained in terms of our energies.' Jo Labanyi, building on Brian Massumi's notion of affect as intensity – an arousal that can be measured physiologically but which happens so fast that consciousness cannot register it – argues that affect is 'doing' at different levels. Sara Ahmed challenges the analytic distinction between affect and emotion on the grounds that it cuts emotions off from the lived experiences of being and having a body. In addition, the distinction between conscious recognition and 'direct' feeling that the model of affect creates cannot be sustained, as that which is not consciously experienced may itself be mediated by past experiences.[42] Ahmed pays attention not to what emotions are but what they do: emotions are viewed not as properties of the self but as produced through the interaction between self and world. Ahmed argues for a concept of subjectivity that is based on relationality with others and with things. In this intersubjective constitution of the subject, emotions 'produce the very surfaces and boundaries that allow the individuals and the social

to be delineated as if they are objects.' Emotions circulate between bodies and shape the surfaces of bodies as well as the boundaries between them. An understanding of emotions as shaped by, and also shaping social structure enables us to perceive the political meaning of emotions and simultaneously how subjects become invested in particular structures. Emotional speech can thus be approached as a bodily act that creates relationality, as moving between bodies. The pain and shame that underlie the words of the speaking actors in Khalili's film do not reduplicate subordination but constitute a powerful political language. They create history as they speak together, relating their story to the stories of other people in the past and present whom they have chosen as interlocutors. Their words 'open up new passages towards new forms of political subjectivisation' and 'rework the frame of our perception and the dynamism of our affects.'[43]

Contrary to the disqualification of native speech, Khalili's work creates a dynamic field, an intensity that is produced through the eradication of the hierarchical construction of knowledge that sees Greece or the South as the object of inquiry and never as the producer of knowledge. Her film constructs communities of words, things and spatiotemporal systems that make us see what subjects have seen. What they have experienced and what the film makes us experience establish new relations between words and visible forms, new forms and meanings.

Equality of speakers is guaranteed in Khalili's work since all subjects are understood and recognised as legitimate speaking subjects. *The Tempest Society* creates a new historicity and poetic modality which produce a setting in which the speakers' speech is not invalidated. Her poetics of politics invent a scene where spoken words become audible by 'overturning the dominant logic that makes the visual the lot of multitudes and the verbal the privilege of a few.'

Writing – poetry, theatre, testimony or autobiography – produces consciousness and new political *names* other than state categories (immigrant, refugee, etc.). In her artistic creation, it is this particular relationship between a poetics of politics and a politics of narrative that establishes a scene for legitimate speakers and achieves its political effect.

1
Yanis Varoufakis, Greek Minister of Finance from January to July 2015, argued that the imposition of austerity measures by the Troika to the southern states of Europe and EU policies turned Europe into 'a democracy free zone by design'. He refers to the then German Minister of Finance at his first meeting with the Eurogroup where, Varoufakis says, he stated that elections should not be allowed to change economic and social policy. Yanis Varoufakis, *Capitalism will eat democracy – unless we speak up*, December 2015, https://www.youtube.com/watch?v=J6Vy1bdhtc0

2
The Family of Man was a photographic exhibition held at the Museum of Modern Art in New York in 1955, a hymn for world unity, celebrating an essential oneness of mankind.

3
The title of Khalili's solo exhibition at Färgfabriken Konsthall in Stockholm in 2016.

4
Jacques Rancière elaborated the critique of a politics of information based on selecting the speaking and reasoning beings who are capable of deciphering the flow of information about anonymous multitudes. Jacques Rancière, *The Emancipated Spectator* (trans. Gregory Elliott), (pp. 25–26), Verso, 2009.

5
Khalili connects *halqa* to Pasolini's cinema of poetry and to his definition of 'civic poetry'. Jonatan Habib Engqvist (interview with B. Khalili), *The Opposite of Voice-Over*, (pp. 25–26), TMG Sthlm, 2016.

6
Demystification, as conceived by Cornel West, 'tries to keep track of the complex dynamics of institutional and other related power structures in order to disclose options and alternatives for transformative praxis'. 'The New Cultural Politics of Difference', by Cornel West, in *The Identity in Question*, John Rajchman (ed.), (pp. 147–171), Routledge, 1995.

7
Rancière, 2009.

8
Yanis Varoufakis, *Capitalism will eat democracy – unless we speak up*, December 2015, www.youtube.com/watch?v=J6Vy1bdhtc0; Christos Papatheodorou, Spyros Sakellaropoulos, Paris Yeros, 'Greece at a Crossroads: Crisis and Radicalization in the Southern European Semi-periphery', *Monthly Review*, May 2012.

9
In 2011, Greeks worked on average 42 hours weekly. The corresponding figure for the total EU-27 was 37 hours. See Papatheodorou, Sakellaropoulos, Yeros, 2012.

10

'Economic crisis, poverty and deprivation in Greece', by Christos Papatheodorou, in *Greek capitalism in crisis: Marxist analyses*, Stavros Mavroudeas (ed.), (pp. 179–195), Routledge, 2014.

11

See Papatheodorou, Sakellaropoulos, Yeros, 2012.

12

Christos Papatheodorou, *op cit*, (pp. 183–187), 2014.

13

'What drives inequality and poverty in the EU? Exploring the impact of macroeconomic and institutional factors', by Yannis Dafermos and Christos Papatheodorou, *International Review of Applied Economics*, Vol. 27, issue 1, 2013; 'Tracking social protection: Origins, path peculiarity, impasses and prospects', by Maria Petmesidou, in *Social policy developments in Greece*, M. Petmesidou & E. Mossialos (eds.), (pp. 25–54), Ashgate, 2006.

14

'Dismantling the Feeble Social Protection System of Greece: Consequences of the Crisis and Austerity Measures', by Sofia Adam and Christos Papatheodorou, in *Challenges to European Welfare Systems*, Klaus Schubert, Paloma de Villota, Johanna Kuhlmann (eds.), (pp. 271–300), Springer, 2016.

15

The broadly used relative poverty definition is 60% of average equivalent disposable national income. As this index is calculated as a percentage of national median income, it is thus affected by changes in the incomes of those in the middle of the distribution.
See Papatheodorou, (pp. 189–190), 2014.

16

See Papatheodorou, (p. 179), 2014.

17

'Religion und Wohlfahrtsstaatlichkeit in Griechenland', by Maria Petmesidou and Periklis Polyzoidis, in *Religion und Wohlfahrtsstaatlichkeit in Europa*, H-R. Reuter & K. Gabriel (eds.), (pp. 177–214), Mohr Siebeck, 2013.

18

'Crisis, Contestation, and Legitimacy in Greece', by Yannis Kallianos, in *Critical Times in Greece: Anthropological Engagements with the Crisis*, Dimitris Dalakoglou & Georgios Agelopoulos (eds.), (pp. 45–55), Routledge, 2018.

19

As Iordanis Psimmenos argues, 'The military junta in Greece (1967–1973), acting on behalf of international capital interests [...] introduced the guest worker system in 1971 for economic and political reasons'. 'The Social Setting of Female Migrant Domestic Workers', by Iordanis Psimmenos, *Journal of Modern Greek Studies*, 35, (pp. 43–66), 2017.

20

Ibid., (p. 46).

21

Servants of Globalization: Women, Migration, and Domestic Work, by Rhacel Salazar Parreñas, Stanford University Press, 2001. 'Gender and the World System: Engaging the Feminist Literature on Development', by Joya Misra, *Cases, Place, and People: World-Systems Studies*, Thomas D. Hall (ed.), Rowman and Littlefield, 2000.

22

'Introduction: Unveiling Domestic Work in Times of Crisis', by Iordanis Psimmenos, in *Journal of Modern Greek Studies*, 35, (pp. 1–16), 2017.

23

'Today let your mops down', Kouneva, 2014.

24

'Nonrecording the "European refugee crisis" in Greece: Navigating through irregular bureaucracy,' by Katerina Rozakou, *Focaal–Journal of Global and Historical Anthropology*, 77, (pp. 36–49), 2017.

25

Ibid., (p. 37).

26

Rozakou uses the term Moria camp to refer to a fragmented, heterogeneous assemblage of diverse agents and jurisdictions. It comprises various sections that fall under the authority of several departments or entire ministries. The Moria camp is not the hotspot; the hotspot is a unit within the camp. The camp also hosts a pre-removal detention centre where deportable people and asylum seekers are held and the Asylum Service supported by EASO officers. 'Access to a Hot Field: A Self-Reflexive Account of Research in the Moria Camp, Lesvos', by Katerina Rozakou, www.law.ox.ac.uk/research-subject-groups/centrecriminology/centreborder-criminologies/blog/2017/11/access-hot-field, 2017.

27

'Exercises of symbiosis in the "humanitarian city": Informal educational practices and governance of the refugee issue since 2016', by Evthymios Papataxiarchis, *Sygxrona Themata*, April-June, 137, (p. 78), 2017.

28

Ibid., (pp. 84–87)

29

Foster cites several reasons for this attraction to anthropology in the art world. Anthropology prizes alterity, takes culture as its object, arbitrates interdisciplinarity, values contextuality and self-critique. 'The Artist As Ethnographer', by Hal Foster, in *The Return of the Real: The Avant-garde at the End of the Century*, (pp. 171–203), MIT Press, 1996.

30

One Place after Another: Site-Specific Art and Locational Identity, by Miwon Kwon, MIT Press, 2002.

31

Ibid., (p. 154).

32

Kwon draws from George Van Den Abbeele's interpretation of Nancy's conceptualisation of community. *Ibid.*, (p. 155).

33

'Bouchra Khalili', by Vivian Ziherl, in *documenta 14: Daybook*, Quinn Latimer and Adam Szymczyk (eds.), Prestel, 2017.

34

Engqvist (interview with B. Khalili), 2016, in 'Bouchra Khalili, Foreign Office,' by Luisa Passerini, 5 September 2015. http://blogbabeproject.eu/bouchra-khalili-foreign-office-2015

35

Engqvist (interview with B. Khalili), 2016; in 'Il cinema di poesia', by Pier Paolo Pasolini, in Empirismo eretico, (pp. 167–187), Garzanti, 1972.

36

Leela Gandhi, *Affective Communities: Anticolonial Thought, Fin-de-Siècle Radicalism, and the Politics of Friendship*, (p. 184), Duke University Press, 2006.

37

For the notion of enunciation as producing a new temporality, see 'On global memory: Reflections on barbaric transmission', by Homi Bhabha, in *Crossing cultures: Conflict, migration, and convergence: The proceedings of the 32nd international congress in the history of art*, J. Anderson (ed.), (pp. 46–56), Miegunyah Press, 2009.

38

'The Fall of the "Purified" Community: Crisis, Transformation & Collective Action in Greece', by Yannis Kallianos, in *The Unfamiliar Journal*, Vol. 2, issue 2, (pp. 30–35), University of Edinburgh, 2012.

39

'To "Lose One's Way" in a City in Crisis: Techniques of Navigating and Walking in Spaces of Disorder', by Yannis Kallianos, in *Remapping 'Crisis': A Guide to Athens*, Myrto Tsilimpounidi & Aylwyn Walsh (eds.), (pp. 86–104), Zero Books, 2014.

40

'Agency of the Street: Crisis, radical politics and the production of public space in Athens 2008–2012', by Yannis Kallianos, in *City: analysis of urban trends, culture, theory, policy, action*, Vol. 17, issue 4, (p. 555), Routledge, 2013.

41

'Doing Things: Emotion, Affect, and Materiality', by Jo Labanyi, *Journal of Spanish Cultural Studies*, (pp. 224–226), Vol. 11, issue 3–4, 2010

42

The Cultural Politics of Emotion, by Sara Ahmed, (pp. 4, 10, 40), Edinburgh University Press, 2004.

43

Rancière, (p. 82–102).

2015

That night and the next two following, we said *No*

108

to those who want a Europe
without politics,

without
popular will,

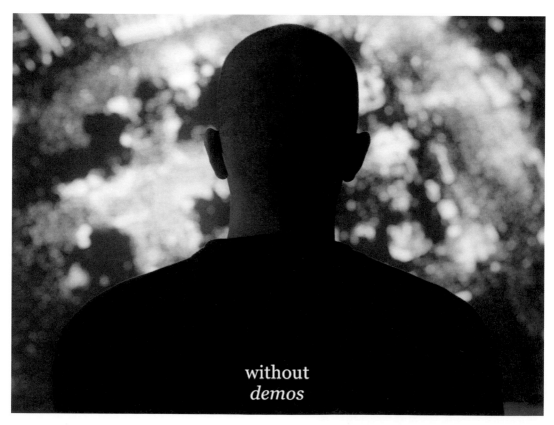

without
demos

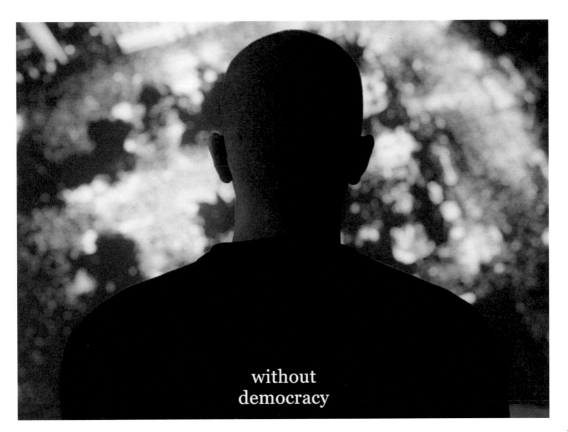

Do you accept the draft agreement submitted by the European Commission,

But was that a question?
I understood:

Do you accept to die a little more,
always more?

Galaxies are sa
of hundreds o

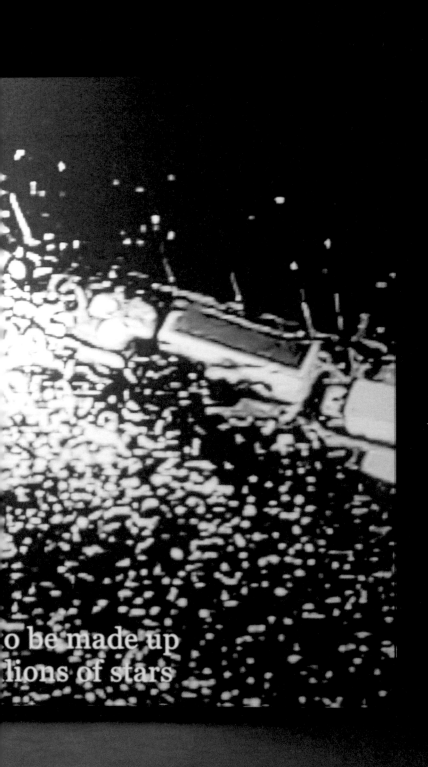

o be made up
lions of stars

Astronomers define the "populations"
of a galaxy as following:

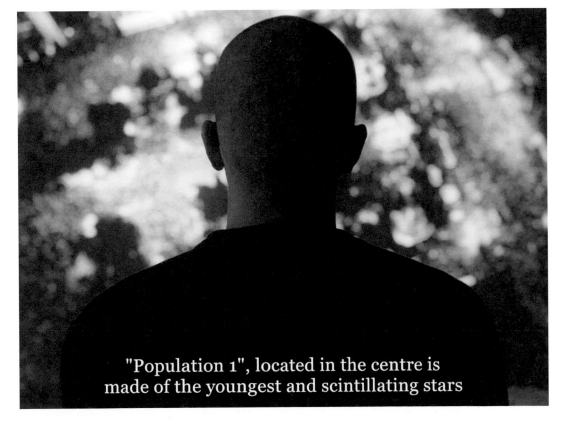

"Population 1", located in the centre is
made of the youngest and scintillating stars

"Population 2",
on the periphery,

is where the dying stars
are extinguished in a glowing colour

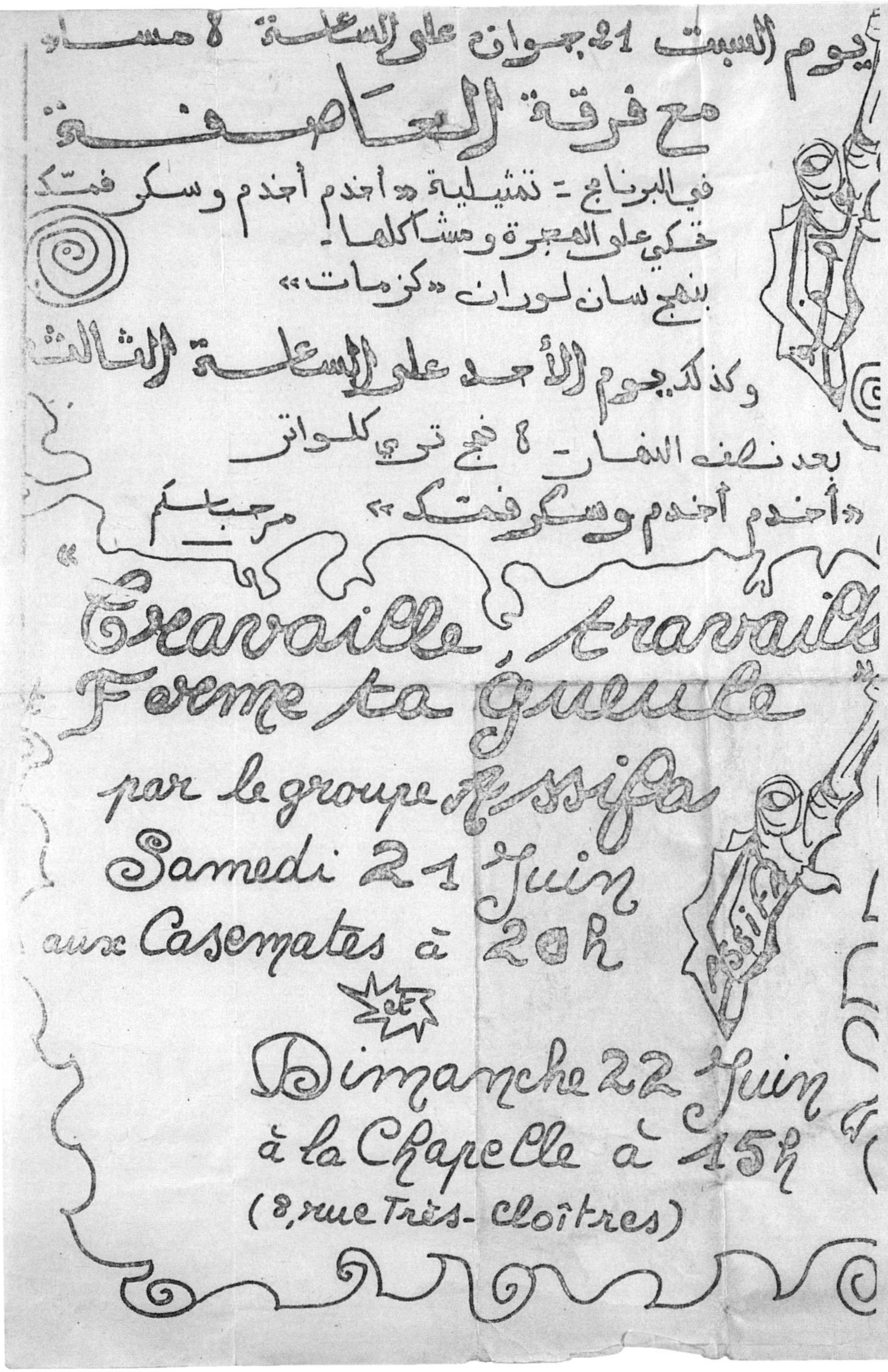

يوم السبت 21 جوان على الساعة 8 مساء

مع فرقة العاصفة

في البرنامج – تمثيلية " اخدم اخدم وسكر فمك "
تحكي على الهجرة ومشاكلها !
بنهج سان لوران " كزمات "

وكذلك يوم الأحد على الساعة الثالثة
بعد نصف النهار – 8 نهج تري كلواتر
" اخدم اخدم وسكر فمك "   مرحبا بكم

Travaille, travaille

Ferme ta gueule

par le groupe R.ssifa

Samedi 21 Juin

aux Casemates à 20h

Dimanche 22 Juin

à la Chapelle à 15h

(8, rue Très-cloîtres)

122

LE SPECTACLE

<u>L HALAKA</u>   dans nos traditions Maghrébines, sont des conteurs
et troubadours, se déplaçant de souks en places publiques.

e conteur des HALAKIS est un homme plein d'humour et de verve.

<u>A TROUPE</u> EL HALAKA est une troupe composée de sept éléments.
Elle est née des besoins de la vie quotidienne des travailleurs Arabes en France. De plus, Elle est née dans le silence
et l'écrasement imposés aux travailleurs immigrés, considérés
comme des bêtes à produire. Cependant, coupés de leur Culture
d'origine, ils ne restent pas impassibles: ils transforment
quotidiennement, par leurs luttes, leur situation.

EL HALAKA inscrit son action et ses objectifs dans la riche
tradition culturelle populaire Arabe.

Par Culture, nous entendons toutes les créations issues de
notre réalité quotidienne, et non le matraquage idéologique
imposé par nos bourgeoisies, que nous considérons comme une
mystification de notre Culture.

Guidés par ces principes, nous inscrivons notre action dans
le cadre d'une RESTITUTION DE L'IDENTITE CULTURELLE IMMIGRES.

Cette identité se définit par le rapprochement à la Culture
dorigine, elle-même transformée par l'expérience de l'Immigration.

<u>A PIECE</u> que nous jouons:"VIVE LA FRANCE, LES IMMIGRES SILENCE", est la
composition d'une série de sketch s expriment le besoin de
luttes et de changements. Ils permettent, aussi, la retrou-
vaille avec la Culture d'origine.

La pièce est beaucoup plus un canevas qu'un texte écrit déjà.
Elle est ouverte, et à l'écoute des faits qui nous entourent
et que nous vivons.

Nous adaptons LE RIRE aux situations que nous jouons - car
nous considérons que le rire est un moyen d'approche intéres-
sant - aussi parceque nous ne pleurons et ne nous lamentons
pas sur"notre sort": nous choisissons d'en rire parceque nous
prenons nos responsabilités.

Cette pièce est le début, nous le souhaitons
à d'autres réalisations à la mesure de nos ambitions, compte tenu de la faiblesse matérielle de
nos moyens, et du chemin à parcourir.... .. ..

EL - HALAKA

Becoming Witnesses: Conversation between Bouchra Khalili, Isavella Alopoudi, Elias Kiama Tzogonas, and Giannis Sotiriou

BOUCHRA

There's a question I always ask
participants in my projects:
Why did you agree to be part of
this project: *The Tempest Society*?

ISAVELLA

That's a good question (laughs).

GIANNIS

I will start, if you don't mind. I'm a visual
art student, so how could I decline your
invitation to participate in this project?
It was so clearly suggesting a strong
artistic approach to a social and a
political context, and that's exactly what
I wanted to engage with. As a Greek,
as an Athenian, and as an artist, I was
also intrigued by your proposal. I wanted
to see how you would approach such
a complex situation and how you
would include our own positions and
perspectives. And that's what I liked
first when you described your project to
me. I thought: I'll be able to finally do
something from which I can learn, and to
which I can contribute at an artistic and
political level.

ISAVELLA

For me, it was exactly the same feeling.
At the time, I had given up working in film
production, although it is what I studied
and wanted to do – support directors
with their projects. But I had lost hope
of contributing to film projects because
our film industry is so devastated, and
I did not want to go back to work on
TV productions. So although you were

proposing that I perform rather than work
on the production aspect of your film,
I said 'yes' to it immediately. I felt that
I could contribute to a project that would
address issues I was reflecting on as
a Greek woman and as a Greek citizen.
Greece is going through a very critical
moment, not only because of the financial
crisis and the refugee crisis. We are living
in troubled times, when everything seems
to be collapsing. To be part of a project
deepening the complexity of the situation
is something I needed, because I thought
that it could help me to deconstruct
that specific reality and that it could help
others to have a better understanding
of the issues at stake.

GIANNIS

And because it is through art, you have
a chance to reach an audience that will
see and listen to unheard and silenced
voices. There's a chance for encounter:
we make a proposal and we offer it to
others to see, listen, reflect, and possibly
learn something.

ELIAS

When we met, my main goal was to
graduate from university. But at the same
time I was also thinking that I would
like to do something that has to do with
theatre. Actually, a little before meeting
you I was offered the opportunity to
be involved in a theatre project, but the
schedule did not fit with the timing of
my final exams, and I eventually declined
that invitation. But when I met you, I liked
you immediately and I liked your project.

And I liked very much that you were very respectful of our commitments, and you immediately took into consideration my class and exam schedule. I remember you were always saying, 'Don't worry Elias, we'll fix it.' And it worked out. We had our five weeks of workshops, our three weeks of shooting, and I graduated as planned. It was amazing. To me, it was the proof that it had to happen.

BOUCHRA
What did you think of the workshop that was based on long conversations, rather than on efficiency of production?

ISAVELLA
For me, it was very interesting from the beginning. I had the opportunity to listen to stories that were so powerful, including ones that eventually were not in the film. The more I listened to those stories, the more I felt that my commitment to the project was going deeper. As an example, at the beginning the story of Al Assifa sounded to me more like a legend. I did not immediately understand how we could turn it into something more personal, or more related to us. But the more we explored it, the more I could understand that this was about us too. And when we met Philippe, our link to Al Assifa became even more obvious and turned into a completely natural connection.

BOUCHRA
Indeed, I was not sure if you could engage with Al Assifa's story, or even if it was relevant to your own lives and experiences. I had already done all the research, and I had scripted and structured material around Al Assifa because even before the invitation extended by documenta I was already working on it for Athens. I already had quite a clear idea on the situation in Greece because I had been closely following it for years. But I also knew that an organic connection to your own lives and experiences needed to be developed, and that the workshop would be a crucial part of our collaboration.

GIANNIS
For me, the workshop was somehow the most important thing that we've done together. It was all about listening and talking. It was very intense and powerful. Without it, it would have been impossible to shoot this film. And I'm not talking about the techniques you taught us about memorising lines and the way to deliver them, or the way we rehearsed the script as if it was a music score. To me the stories we heard and discussed were the most important thing. I remember that during the first days, Isavella and myself were not talking that much. We were very impressed by what Elias was telling us about being a black man in Greece, although he grew up in this country.

BOUCHRA
So what did you learn?

GIANNIS
Well, of course we knew that racism exists within Greek society, but it is a completely different thing when people experiencing it tell it in front of you, when you realise that even your childhood memories are marked by discrimination. It was like a punch in my face. After each session, Isavella and myself were thinking that we did not have such stories to tell because we are white, we live in 'our' country, we are privileged. You know, I meet people, I read books. You certainly remember that when we started the workshop I was reading that book by Angela Davis about race and class. But listening to Elias and others telling those stories with their own words and their own voices, suddenly it became real. I became a witness, eventually asking myself: what I can do to change that?

BOUCHRA
Do you mean that you realised what 'white privilege' means?

GIANNIS
I actually realised that Elias's position in Greek society was not that of a victim, but rather that it was subverting the

system's narrative. He was resisting the pressure of a system that rejects people like him, people who do not fit with what is considered here as a citizen or a member of the community.

BOUCHRA
I remember that you mentioned that you often had bad dreams during the first days of the workshop.

GIANNIS
Yes, many, every night.

ISAVELLA
Yes, during the first days of the workshop, I too was having bad dreams every night about being caught at borders, about police violence, about fleeing a war. What had the biggest impact on me was getting so close to Elias and to the others who told us their stories. They were becoming our friends and we knew them then. We could not escape that violence and we had to face it and interrogate it, and also to interrogate our position with regards to it. So for me too it was the most important part of the work we've done together, because this is when I learnt the most, both about Al Assifa and about how individuals around us, who were getting close to us, are resisting racism and injustice. Filming, in comparison, was so easy and enjoyable. But we needed those weeks of intense conversations and rehearsals to fully understand and get fully conscious of what we were doing together.

ELIAS
I remember one day during the workshop thinking that I was talking too much. I felt like 'I'm living in a house, and now I'm spitting on it.' But I quickly understood that as a Greek citizen it is part of my duty to address the issues we have to solve collectively.

BOUCHRA
For me, it was also very difficult, because I'm not Greek and I don't live in Athens, although I spent several months here. I was afraid to make comments that could sound offensive. I was also constantly asking myself about my own position with regards Greek history, Greek society, and its current situation.

ISAVELLA
But we were not only addressing the Greek situation. We were talking about issues that were relevant to Greece, but that were also relevant to many different contexts. After all, we were exploring what radical equality could mean. So I never thought that you were criticising Greece, but rather that we were committed to facing factual situations from which we could reflect on how to achieve equality.

ELIAS
Nevertheless, I believe I could have been more diplomatic during the workshops. I realised later that I was sometimes speaking with anger. But still I wanted to talk about my position as an 'Afro-Greek' and I had to address it openly and frankly. And because I was given that opportunity, I used it. However, I was surprised that Giannis and Isavella were so keen to listen, and they were indeed listening carefully. I had the feeling that there was a great sense of respect in the way that they were listening. So I also understood that Isavella and Giannis needed to hear what I had to say, that they needed to understand. I also felt confident because I knew that you (Bouchra), you knew very well what we were talking about, I mean me, Katarina, Malek – because you're from North Africa, from a former colonised country, and because you lived as an immigrant in the West and have done so many works on the subject.

BOUCHRA
We did this work a few months ago. Now that you've seen the film, do you think that it reflects the way it was produced?

ISAVELLA
Although the workshop was very organic in its development, the material you gave us to perform was very carefully scripted and precise. Similarly, I found the film very

128

carefully structured and somehow very close to what I imagined when we were filming. I saw it as a reflection of how we worked together. But strangely I found it more related to the workshop than to the shooting, because in the same way that at times during the workshop we were the 'storytellers' and at other times we were the 'listeners' and the 'witnesses', in the film it operates exactly the same way. And just as during the workshops, we were all sharing and using the same platform.

GIANNIS

If I had not seen your work during the workshop, it would have been more mysterious. But because you showed us your work, and because we could also discuss it, from the first day of shooting I had a clear idea of what we were doing. And when I was not being filmed, I was still on the set. You let us watch the making of some scenes and even look with you at the monitor. So when I saw the film for the first time, I thought that it was very close to what we experienced on the set.

ELIAS

Yes, it's true. You were not hiding the monitor from us. So we were watching you directing scenes, and we were whispering to each other, 'what beautiful framing, look at the colours, look at Isavella, she looks amazing.' We were witnessing the making of the film and not being limited to our role as performers. The only thing that surprised me was that everything looked bigger on the screen. The frames also impressed me. On the big screen, I could see that they were not random at all, but very carefully composed. On the set, I also did not realise the power of the words we were saying.

BOUCHRA

So what you are saying is that it never entered your mind that it could end up being a bad movie? (laughs).

ELIAS

On the set, it was like watching a painter working: I like that stroke, and I like that one too.

BOUCHRA

I understand, you're also a painter. But a good movie is not a sum of nice shots.

ELIAS

You're right. But we observed you a lot. We could see that you knew what you were doing. So we were absolutely confident.

BOUCHRA

I appreciate that very much, because I needed to feel that sense of mutual trust. The film was very clear in my mind. But at the same time I wanted you to be completely involved in it, and your opinion was so important to me. I was not performing the role of 'the director', and you were not performing the role of 'the actors'.

ISAVELLA

We felt very much included throughout the whole process, and I also felt I was part of a group. Not in the sense of the usual shooting: we perform the 'troupe' behaviour, and when it's done, no one keeps in touch.

ELIAS

At first, I thought that you would give me indications and I would do what you want. But that is not what our relationship was about: you were listening to us. And that's also why I felt very much included: I was listened to and I was heard. And I felt even more included when Philippe came and joined us on the set. It was such a magical moment. I admired Al Assifa so much because they rebelled against injustice. And I admire Philippe a lot because he was not an immigrant worker, but still stood in solidarity with them and fought with them for their rights. He intrigued me a lot before meeting him: why did he spend six years of his life fighting for others people's rights? And when I saw him, I understood immediately: he believed

in it. He could not stay silent. I wish
I could have met Geneviève, Mokhtar, Ali,
Djilali, and all the others. So it was even
more than feeling a belonging to a group.
I felt like I was part of a larger history.

GIANNIS

I felt exactly the same meeting Philippe.
I realised: this is true. This was real. During
the workshop, the connection to Al Assifa
was still a bit theoretical to me, although
I understood that you had a clear idea
of how to articulate those resonances
between that story and our lives and
experiences. But seeing Philippe standing
next to us, it suddenly illuminated the
whole process: the connections we were
making between Al Assifa and our stories
were relevant and consistent: there was
a possible dialogue throughout time and
geography. That was such a great moment.

BOUCHRA

Philippe was extremely moved. If you
remember, when he arrived on the set
there was a monitor displaying footage
from a super 8 short film showing excerpts
of a performance by Al Assifa in an
occupied factory. He'd never seen that
material before. He saw it for the first
time on our set. He was there, standing,
watching himself and Mokhtar dancing
together almost forty years before.
But this was happening 'here and now':
in Athens, in 2016. And that's when he
understood why I asked him to join us
and to share the stage with you.

ISAVELLA

Sharing the stage with Philippe was literally
like seeing a ghost of history appearing
and sitting with us, joining us to somehow
continue a timeless story. And that's exactly
how it looks in the film. It is also at that
specific moment that I felt that I was not
only part of a group, but more of a collective.
I can't find a better word to describe that
feeling. Somehow, I felt that the shooting
was not the end of this project but only its
beginning. And I mean it at different levels.

ELIAS

After a shooting, you would expect that
people wouldn't stay in touch. But I knew
that this won't happen with this project.
Isavella, Giannis, and myself, we became
friends, and we still hang out together.
And we stay in touch with you.

GIANNIS

When my schoolmates were asking me
what I was doing in that film, I told them,
this is the best thing I've ever done. And
even when I had not memorised my lines
properly, I was not worried or anxious.
I felt very confident because I knew that
everyone would help me and that you
would support me. As Isavella and Elias
were saying, it definitely was not like how
one expects a film shoot to be.

ELIAS

But to me, watching it with you guys and
watching the film alone were completely
different experiences. I must say that
watching it alone was even more powerful.
It is there that I saw the film for itself, and
not us, or our friendship, in the film.

BOUCHRA

Last question: do you have a message
for Philippe?

ISAVELLA

I felt so touched when we had that dinner
in Exarchia. Talking to him, I got the feeling
that this was not an art project, but that
it was about his life.

BOUCHRA

That's why I did not want to interfere.
I knew that you could speak French, even
though I realised it only when Philippe
joined us (laughs). I thought that at that
point you had to 'meet' Philippe without
my intervention, that it was about you
three and him. So I loved watching you
translating for Elias and Giannis, as well
as becoming Philippe's translator during
those days. For me, it was like a metaphor
of the film and its connection to Al Assifa:
we were translating a forgotten language,
bringing it back to life.

130

ISAVELLA

Honestly, I was surprised that I could remember some French (laughs). I enjoyed translating for Philippe so much. I also kept that piece of paper on which he wrote a message for us. And we also have a recording of his voice. That's my message for him: his words and his voice are with us.

GIANNIS

I want to ask him something: I want to make a black and white portrait of his face and of his hands. Please, ask him to give me a photo of himself with his hands visible. I want to paint that portrait. I have to.

ELIAS

I've spoken with some Afro-Greek friends here in Athens who are performers and activists. I shared Al Assifa's story with them. Now, we're discussing how we can use that legacy. I want to keep Philippe informed of how we intend to do it in Athens.

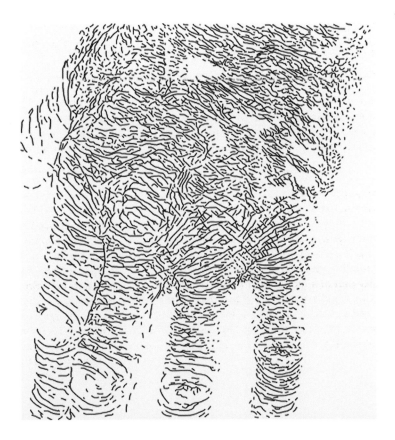

One and the other
from *Les Tiers Idées*, Geneviève Clancy and Philippe Tancelin

One, a smile on his face, is wearing a tie…
We have seen him already somewhere, he looks like…
    The other, a carnation in his buttonhole,
is wearing a tie… We've seen him around already,
he looks like…
—   Hello?
—   Hello!
—   Is that the French Minister of Foreign Affairs?
—   Mr D., State Secretary on the phone.
—   I'm the African Minister at the Department
    of Labour.
—   Delighted, how are you?
—   Not very happy.
—   Not very happy?
—   Guess what, I've received complaints from
    your government about the shipment of tomatoes
    I sent you.
—   I heard about it, but rest assured, it was a
    diplomatic mistake. I hope you're not calling
    me for that?
—   No, I have a proposition for you: it's strong,
    it's robust, it works and works, and it keeps
    its mouth shut.
—   You're talking about your workers I guess,
    so send me some, let's say…

There are hundreds arriving by boat. Just like
the economic markets that apply for citrus fruits,
oil, and other products of exchange, immigration —
or the market of labour force — is settled on
agreements between governments solely concerned
with making profit.
    In 1972, the Marcellin-Fontanet circulars were
promulgated, and it was presented like a resolution
to improve and regulate the conditions of entry
of migrant workers. It was in reality a reinforcing
of police control as well as a form of enslavement
by the managerial class. Against those circulars
the resistance of the migrant workers was organised.
Hunger strikes took place all over France, despite
hundreds of expulsions.

AFRICAN MINISTER: All right then, they'll be on the next boat.

FRENCH MINISTER: Good, but I'd like them to keep quiet because for a while now I've been noticing protests, strikes.

AFRICAN MINISTER: Don't worry, I selected them. As for the blunders, they're only the actions of a few lefty agitators, all French by the way, and some priests who've strayed from Christ's path, all of which you'll be able to take care of, I'm sure.

PRESS RELEASE: In Paris, several Arab and Mauritian migrant workers carry on their hunger strikes in two churches to fight against the Marcellin-Fontanet circulars. Some French people from the neighbourhood as well as members of the Committee for the defence of immigrant workers' lives and rights are behind them.

A COMRADE FROM THE THEATRE COMPANY: Ladies and gentlemen, tonight (January 74) at the cinema 'Quatorze Juillet', where we've just performed the play *Ça travaille…*, migrant workers are on strike, a few metres from here. Some of our comrades who've just performed for you are also taking part in that hunger strike. One of them, who took part in the sit-in we organised at the Department of Labour, is going to share with you the latest information we have, as well as the response from the Ministry.
     Tonight at the 'Quatorze Juillet', Al Assifa and the comrades of the theatre company who began a hunger strike in solidarity with the migrant workers, invite you to a meeting in support of the strikers, tomorrow, Sunday, 2pm at the Church of St O…

FRENCH MINISTER: I'll see you very soon, dear colleague, it will be a pleasure to welcome you to Paris.

AFRICAN MINISTER: See you soon.

(The African Minister stays.
The French Minister leaves…)

AFRICAN MINISTER: Come on, get a move on!

THE ACTORS: They carry cardboard boxes on their heads, the workers leaving for France. We don't see them, but do we need to see them? You, you're Citroën; you, Chausson; you, Renault; and you, the mines in the north. Your face doesn't matter, you're not here to think but to keep your mouth shut.

AFRICAN MINISTER: And I'm warning you, our government has made a big leap forward… Anything you do right, the people will say: 'Your government is good'; anything you do wrong, they will say: 'Your government is bad'; and that's not good for your government… When you're not on your own turf, you shut your mouth… no politics.

THE ACTORS: They shut their mouth. They work, they work and…

FRENCH MINISTER: Come on, come forward now, you're in France. Gentlemen, before we unload you, let me share with you our great pleasure in welcoming you onto our territory. You came to France to work, and you will work the French way. Gradually, gentlemen, you will learn to speak French, and you'll end up thinking in French.
    From land to land you didn't have a chance to see the sea, packed as you were in the holds of boats. Parcels, goods, this side up, a name, a single name on the package, that of the company to which you'll be sent. Of all that, what did you know, you and the others, who thought about other things… Paris, France, it's going to be…

The Foreign Legion for example…

FRENCH MINISTER: Come closer boy, you're going to enter the Legion. You know what that is?

WORKER: A job for an honest man, with prospect.
— Very good, my boy… Are you married?
— Yes.
— You are not married… Children?

— Three.
— You don't have children, you hear me? Here
   you're a virgin… You'll be in for five years,
   you knew that, right…
— But sir, I was told…
— You've been told nothing. The Legion is the
   Legion… There you go, lad, on your way to Chad…
— It's true, he hasn't been told anything…

The Foreign Legion has opened in Mauritius back
rooms where they recruit. It promises the earth
to workers whom poverty forces to emigrate, telling
them that in France, in the Legion, they will earn
hundreds of thousands of francs, and that their
future is assured. We, the comrades from Al Assifa,
we've seen those workers coming from Mauritius,
turning up at the Gare du Nord around midnight,
in coaches, after having been brought in transit
through Belgium. The men were exhausted, completely
lost, as they realised during those first minutes
in Paris that they had been duped, bought like
cattle. Some had sold all their belongings to pay
for the trip. Those the Foreign Legion didn't want
because they were too small, not strong enough,
or no longer corresponded to the legionnaire's type
found themselves wandering in Paris without papers,
without money; some were picked up, half-starved,
sleeping rough at the entrance to the sewers, or
in the metro. We saw them arriving around midnight,
dozens at a time at the Gare du Nord. They gathered,
then gradually organised themselves to fight.
    To fight and to say, through the voice of
a chorus, on stage, one evening:

The wolves from here and the jackals from
over there have agreed to crush us in their
infernal machines.
    We have become goods.
    We are the foreigners, the migrants.
    We are the workers.
    We are the men, the slaves of modern times.
    Against racism, against exploitation, we
are ready to pay with our blood, we are ready
to pay with our life, so as to not have to pay
with our humanity.

In The
they were welcome

loniki,
the workers' house

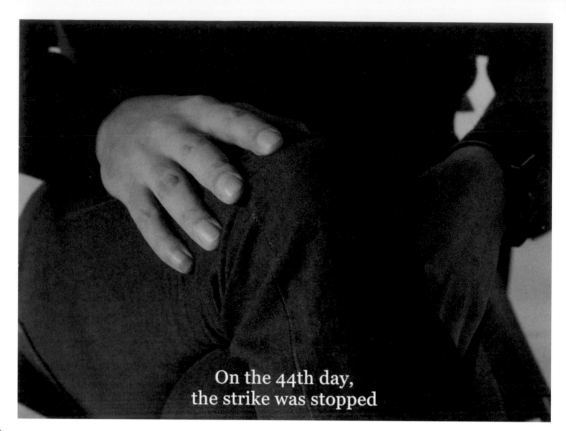

On the 44th day,
the strike was stopped

with the promise that our demands
will be discussed in parliament:

The work permit
was never granted

But the new law on health insurance
has benefited everyone

143

When one struggles for rights,
these rights are for the whole of society

APPEL AUX TRAVAILLEURS BELGES ET IMMIGRES

Des travailleurs arabes de France présentent une pièce
de théâtre sur la vie des immigrés :
    "Travaille, travaille et tais-toi !"
Le

Après les luttes menées en France par les travailleurs
immigrés pour leurs droits, ils ont fait cette pièce de
théâtre qu'ils ont jouée dans toutes les villes de France.

Cette pièce de théâtre arrive après les luttes contre
le racisme, contre l'exploitation, contre les attaques
racistes, pour les droits au travail, à la dignité et la
carte de travail ; elle a aidé les immigrés à s'unir entre
eux et avec les travailleurs français.

Tous les travailleurs et intellectuels sont invités
à venir nombreux

Des travailleurs arabes

Editeur Responsable : William Roelants
            Rue Saint Quentin 65

            1040   BRUXELLES

بمناسبة . غرة ماي

مهرجان شعبي يوم (السبت ١ ماي)
على الساعة الثامنة والنصف مع
فرقة العاصفة بباريس
٨ نهج بيار ليرميت ميترو باربيس

FêTe PoPuLaire

à l'occasion du 1ᵉ MAI
organisée par la troupe ELASSIFA

SAMEDI 1ᵉʳ MAI

à 20ʰ30 à la salle saint Bruno
8 Rue Pierre L'Hermite.
Metro BARBES

الرجاء الحضور إلى مركز

AVENUE SARAGOSSE البحث واللقاء

لمشاهدة تمثيلية عنوانها " اخدم واسكت "

و ذلك يوم الاحد ٢٧ ابريل على

الساعة السادسة مساء

الدعوة موجهة لجميع العمال

المهاجرين .

الدخول مجانا

VOUS ETES TOUS INVITES.....
A LA PIECE DE THEATRE JOUEE PAR DES TRAVAILLEURS IMMIGRES

"CA TRAVAILLE,CA TRAVAILLE ET CA FERME SA GUEULE!!"

AU CENTRE RENCONTRE ET RECHERCHE
AVENUE DE SARAGOSSE

DIMANCHE 27 AVRIL A 18 heures précises

—entrée gratuite—

* ΓΚΑΖΜΕΝΤ

*

*

2011

ΑΛ ΛΕΞΙ

ANI

* KATEPINA

A

α υπήρξε το θέατρο της ζω
ς «είμαι Αθηναίος». Η Αθ
πρασίνου και την κρίση χρ
Ελλάδας. Αλλά το πιο σημ
σης, από το εσωτερικό της
μα μετανάστευσης και προ

ιγότερο από είκοσι χρό
λεις της νότιας Ευρώπης
νας προήλθε από «αλλο
προκαλεί δυσπιστία και
ις σε προβλήματα που μ
σφαίρα της φαντασίας. Ο Α

Most importantly, o
is the result of co

μου. Αν κάποιος με ρωτ

α είναι μοναδική, όχι μόν

υς. Είναι μια πόλη στην

τικό, η σύγχρονη Αθήνα

ύρας και από το εξωτερικ

ατι το πιο τραγικό.

α, η Αθήνα εξελίχθηκε

α τελευταία είκοσι πέν

. Και άλλοι συνεχίζουν

γκρούσεις, έκπληξη και

temporary Athens
ς πριν είκοσι χρόνια υπr
ual migrations,

λος είναι ένας καθρέφτης

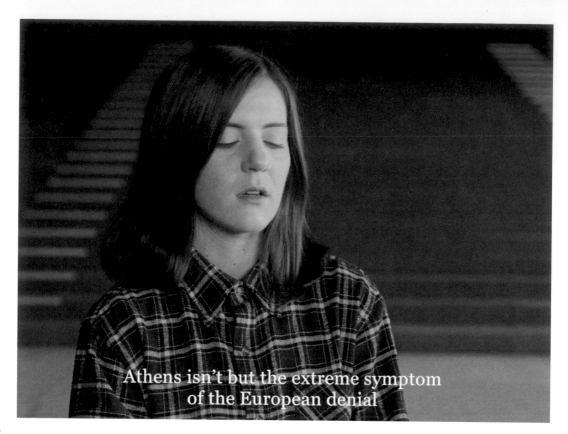

Athens isn't but the extreme symptom
of the European denial

And yet,
I repeat,

I was born at the Alexandra
maternity hospital in Athens

I count the time
on my skin

I have lived in Athens
for twenty-six years

and I have created
my own calendar

AL ASSIFA

THEATRE

la vie
de chateau

tous les samedi 20h30 dimanche16 h .

8 BIS RUE PIERRE L'ERMITE METRO BARBES

tel ode 03 26

LA VIE DE CHATEAU

MILLIONS D'HOMMES LOIN DE LEURS TERRES ,NOTRE VOIX EST GROSSE DE CELLE DE NOS FRERES LA BAS ET DE NOTRE EXIL ACHETE ICI. L'EXPRESSION SUR UNE SCENE NOUS APPARTIENT ,TOUT COMME DANS LA RUE QUAND NOUS MANIFESTONS, NOUS NE CESSERONS DE LES MENER DE FRONT AVEC L'AIDE ET LA SOLIDARITE DE TOUS CEUX QUI JUSQU'ALORS FURENT A NOS COTES.

DU CHANTIER,DE L'ENTREPRISE, DE L'UNIVERSITE , OU LES UNS ET LES AUTRES CAMARADES DE LA TROUPE AL ASSIFA ,NOUS TRAVAILLONS ,JUSQU'AU THEA-TRE QUE NOUS CREONS A BARBES. CE SONT LES VOIX ET GESTES DONT ON NOUS FAIT LA VIE.

ASSIFA POUR NOS DROITS ,ASSIFA POUR NOS CULTURES , ASSIFA POUR NOTRE HUMANITE SUR TOUS LES FRONTS.

Imprimerie Gilles Tautin
4, passage Dieu 75020 Paris

ملايين من الرجال غرباء عن أرضنا في الهجرة صوتنا يتغوى بصوت اخواننا في البلد . نملك عبرتنا في المسرح او في الشارع بالمظاهرات وسنتابع هادا مع جميع الذين بجانبنا . من الشانطيي الى المعمل ومن الكلية نضال اخرجت منه العاصفة ، عاصفة تملى كل الجبهات

» هادي غربة ولا هبال «

لكل مشيد الساعة الثامنة والنصف وكل احد الساعة الرابعة
– قاعة دسان بريشو ، –

Calling the Ghosts: Conversation Between Bouchra Khalili and Omar Berrada

OMAR

How did you first come across Al Assifa? Moroccan-born whose parents emigrated to france, what personal relationship do you have with this particular story and its legacy?

BOUCHRA

To answer your question, I need to give a sense of context. I have inherited a double history: the history of anti-colonial struggle and the history of immigration. My mother was born the very week that negotiations for the independence of Morocco began. My father was born colonised, six years earlier. Both belong to a generation that hoped that in formerly colonised countries independence would be followed by progressive regimes. You and I were both born at a time when that hope was already shattered. What remained were the stories. And that's how I first heard of the MTA.

Years later, for whatever reason – but it must have been a good one – maybe a resonance with a current context – I remembered the story of the MTA. I started to look at it more in depth. And that's how I realised that not only was it the first autonomously organised group of North African workers in France, but its members created the first theatre troupe that brought together North African workers and French students. What immediately interested me with Al Assifa was its perspective on art coming from immigrant workers, who identified primarily as activists but who nevertheless were rethinking art as a space for the civic, as a platform from which belonging was freed from nationalism in favour of radical solidarity and radical equality.

OMAR

The Tempest Society seems to me, in part, an exercise in resurrecting a political moment along with some of its protagonists, like Mokhtar Bachiri – a resurrection that relies on what I would call a 'complex evocation', involving photographic documentation, a montage of narratives, the enfleshment of history into bodies and voices, and a certain reflexivity in the telling. Do you see this as a work of history? Of testimony? Of critique? Of translation? Do you feel any kind of 'responsibility' to tell this story?

BOUCHRA

I don't know if I can call it a resurrection, unless I literally follow Godard's motto: 'Cinema authorised Orpheus to look back without causing Eurydice's death.'[1] In *Histoire(s) du Cinéma*, he also stated – quoting Saint Paul – that 'the image will come at the time of the resurrection.' But an image in wait for a resurrection is an image in latency. It is the resurrection that allows it to become a representation. My task is simpler and much more modest. It starts from the awareness that the whole story cannot be reconstituted. It is lost. This is a matter of fact. So the question becomes: what can we do with what remains? If you remember the ending of *Foreign Office*,[2] Inès says 'we have inherited only disenchantment and history in pieces.' Therefore the question is: how do we combine those fragments, not in order to tell the whole story but to bring together what can be shared – knowing

162

and acknowledging that there are missing parts. And how can we share it? In the same film, Inès quotes Kateb Yacine speaking about the French language in Algeria as the spoils of war. But images, traces, sounds, stories in pieces can also be seen as spoils of war, so how do we bring all the fragments together? How can we turn them into one food basket that belongs to everyone and that can be shared by all? That's what an image is for me: a combination of fragments that can circulate among the ones in need of the missing image. It won't replace the whole image, but it can help figure out what can be said about it.[3]

OMAR

There is a complex choreography of bodies throughout the film. Sometimes they are facing us; sometimes they are facing each other; or they are shot from the back, watching something. There is a scene in which they are holding other faces to their own, like masks of the original protagonists of Al Assifa – they literally bear someone else's face. For you, what is a body in a film? Who does it belong to? What does it stand for?

BOUCHRA

The choreography is what is produced by the cuts, by 'montage' as the epitome of cinematic language, and by 'mise en scène' as a praxis of representation. I am using French terms here because they are more precise. Montage is a combination of cuts producing a conceptual framework for the representation of time, space, and of course bodies. Mise en scène is more confusing: it can be misunderstood as a 'fabrication' or a 'manipulation'. But what I am referring to is the opposite. It is a conception of 'staging' inherited from the golden age of French film criticism as embodied by 'Les Cahiers du Cinéma' and its dream team gathered around André Bazin: Eric Rohmer, François Truffaut, Jean-Luc Godard, Jean Douchet, among others.

This conception of mise en scène upholds the concept that the viewer's location is an integral part of the space of representation. The question of the body in my work is therefore fully connected to presence, self-representation, montage, and mise en scène. In all of my works, the body is accompanied by a sense of opacity, a sense of presence-absence. Bodies are not only physical presences: they are voices calling ghosts to join them.

In The Tempest Society, the scene you're referring to is literally a metaphor of this conception of the representation of the body in my work: they are representing themselves while simultaneously representing the absentees and the ones who can't speak. Therefore, montage and mise en scène become tools that facilitate the circulation of speech among bodies, present and absent, allowing for the picture of a potential community to come into being, a potential community in which the viewers are included.

The choreography is also rooted in very concrete details. For instance the location where the entire film was shot is a former factory which, every summer, turns into a theatre to host the 'Athens Festival'. We filmed during the winter, so it was completely empty. What struck me when I first visited it are the dozens of windows, which would allow filming in natural light, as well as the beautiful spatial contrast: on one side, the staircase in the darkness, on the other, the stage bathed in light. The staircase is a closed space. The stage is an open space from which windows can be seen, involving an off-screen space: the world. Therefore the mise en scène was obvious, since the space itself was offering a dialectic of representation: the performers and witnesses, and the nature of their functions following the permutation of those two spaces – the staircase and the stage.

This is what defined the shots and their editing from the start, because I always film with the final edit in mind. That way

I don't need to accumulate too much material. What was filmed is in the final edit, because I already had the whole structure in mind, and this dialectics of representation was at its core.

OMAR

The actors of Al Assifa played their own parts, performed their own lives. In Philippe Tancelin's words, 'they perform and they have not changed from the street to the stage.' To what extent might this apply to your film's protagonists?

BOUCHRA

They are Isavella, Elias, Giannis. They speak for themselves from their own positions. But they are also a potential multitude, the multitude of the absentees. Various scenes suggest this constant movement back and forth from the singular to the collective and vice versa. Later in the film, Katarina appears on stage, as a guest. But she does not tell her story. She reads it from a book by Gazmend Kapllani, *My Name Is Europe*. What she reads is her own story as written by Gazmend. His book is the account of his own immigration from Albania to Greece in the early nineties, but it is more generally a meditation on the 'foreigner' and his becoming a 'citizen' within a new society. The narration includes 'documentary' accounts of other stories of immigration, among which are those of Katarina and Elias.

So at one point, and for a few minutes, Elias is no longer a member of the group but a guest. He is with Katarina on the stage, and he too reads his own story from Gazmend's book. At that moment, Isavella and Giannis listen to him without interrupting. However, they had introduced the scene by reading a letter sent to me by Gazmend. So at that moment they are witnesses while also representing Gazmend. But they also represent me, because the letter was sent to me, and they are reading it on my behalf because I'm absent from the stage – but through that reading I am present, just like Gazmend. So the scene becomes a

reflection on authorship: who speaks? Katarina, Elias, Gazmend, me? We are all there together. Eventually, what is suggested here is a circulation of speech as defined by Pier Paolo Pasolini and his cinema of poetry: the encounter of equal voices. They are located in specific bodies, but because they are merged, they can call for a larger body to come together. It is not by chance that Pasolini is mentioned in the first chapter of the film: the civic poet and the theorist of the cinema of poetry, which *The Tempest Society* is also about.

OMAR

By staging the relations between times and geographies (for instance Paris in the 1970s, Athens today), your work forcefully affirms that solidarity must be transnational and trans-temporal (Elias says: 'When one struggles, one meets others who struggle elsewhere, in all the corners of the world.' Compare this to Thomas Sankara: 'We wish to be the heirs of all the revolutions of the world.') In doing so, your work calls attention to historical continuities in oppression, or what we might call a colonial continuum, under which we are still living. I see this work (and much of your work) as a carefully crafted indictment of the persisting coloniality of power. Would you agree?

BOUCHRA

I would rather talk about the persisting forms of resistance invented individually and collectively. What my work examines above all is the language of those forms of resistance, the collective potential that arises from singular gestures of resistance.

In the first chapter of *The Tempest Society*, on the table on which the 'script' is unfolded from a combination – a montage – of pictures, one can see Antonio Gramsci. He is present, next to pictures of Al Assifa, Pasolini and Panagoulis, as well as pictures of the occupation of Syntagma Square in

2011 by Greek citizens and in 2014 by Syrian refugees.

In this continuum of resistance, what interests me above all is how forms of resistance permanently reinvent themselves. As an optimist, I have to be prepared to 'organise pessimism', so I choose to view history as a long chain of forms of resistance that still resonate 'here and elsewhere', 'yesterday and today', allowing us to picture a potential tomorrow.

OMAR

I am wondering if you can elaborate on the necessity of (spatial and temporal) distance. Could you have made a work around Al Assifa in Paris?

BOUCHRA

It would have been a completely different film. I did consider it at the very beginning of the research process, as you know, since you were involved at a very early stage of this project. But soon after, I started to follow very closely the situation in Greece.

I literally became obsessed. Gilles Deleuze often said that to belong to the left is to perceive the horizon first, in order to be able to understand what is happening on your street corner. I had the feeling that what Greece was going through was crucial for the future of Europe: the memorandum, the violent austerity measures, what was later described as 'the refugee crisis' – although as Moroccans we both know that it started a long time ago on the North African coasts with the Schengen Agreement that offered freedom of movement for Europeans while closing the doors of Europe to the neighbouring countries. That's how I got involved with Greece, and that's how I realised that there could not be any other place for this project than Athens.

The other reason is that I always felt a strong sympathy for the Greek people, maybe because as a Moroccan I also inherited a history of struggle against colonialism and neo-colonialism, and a history of emigration that has produced a powerful diasporic culture, among other similarities. Living and working in Athens for half a year made that feeling of sympathy and solidarity even stronger. That being said, the point was never about producing analogies between French society in the seventies and contemporary Greek society. It was about reactivating forms of resistance. If Al Assifa's experience still has relevance within the current context of Greece, the Mediterranean area, Europe, and hopefully elsewhere, it is because what is timely is the need for equality and solidarity. And Greece – Athens in particular – is the place where the concepts of civic equality and of theatre were invented, along with the rich links between them. That's what convinced me that there could be no better place than Athens for this project.

OMAR

Toward the beginning of *The Tempest Society*, we are told that Al Assifa was a group that seized the soul of theatre to achieve its fight for immigrant and workers' rights. Art is enlisted as a means for political struggle. How do you view your own art in this light?

BOUCHRA

You're asking a crucial question, because I am not an activist. But am I an artist? I often ask myself. I am not sure. My mother says that I'm a writer working with images. But I guess she says that because she still wishes that one day I'll stop wasting my time with image making, exhibition making, and finally write a book. Maybe I'm just like a child: I ask too many questions, and my way of doing it is to draft them with pictures and sounds. In the end, the questions I ask myself may be boiled down to the following: what is this form of poetry that originates in persistent lives?

Genet said it better than I could when he defined the poetry of revolutionaries: 'If we accept this idea, that the revolutionary enterprise of a man or of a people originates in their poetic genius, or, more precisely, that this enterprise is the inevitable conclusion of poetic genius, we must reject nothing of what makes poetic exaltation possible... because poetry contains both the possibility of a revolutionary morality and what appears to contradict it.'

Working on Al Assifa, taking inspiration from it, and transporting it to Greece was my way to examine how this revolutionary morality, and the possibility of a poetic exaltation within the chaotic world in which we live, can still exist and still resist.

OMAR
For obvious reasons, *The Tempest Society* foregrounds theatre as an art form. It made me wonder how, as a filmmaker, you view your work's relation to the theatre.

BOUCHRA
I was a member of a theatre group between the ages of sixteen and twenty-one. I was 'chosen' to perform, though I never enjoyed performing. I was much more interested in the process of developing the performances, which were often based on combining existing material, improvisation, choreography, collective conversations. I did enjoy the collective aspect of theatre making. And during those years, I saw many good plays by Ariane Mnouchkine, Peter Brook, Pina Bausch, among others. But, at the same time, I was never a theatre-goer. The truth is that I was already spending a lot of time in art house cinemas and at the French Cinémathèque. I was always much more interested in theatricality as produced by cinematic language, for instance in Fassbinder's movies, in some of Godard's films from the seventies, in Straub and Huillet's films, and some of Pasolini's movies such as *Porcile* or *Teorema*. Not to mention films from the early age of cinema. If one looks at films by Chaplin or Keaton, the body is always located at the centre of the frame. The frame is a sort of extension of the stage, a nomadic stage that follows the movements of the body while remaining perfectly static and frontal. Both Chaplin and Keaton came from the theatre and both were extraordinary performers, or should I say athletes? I have always admired performers who are skilled at making precise gestures. I guess it's not by chance if many of the non-professional actors in my films have in common an extreme precision at performing very specific gestures: moving pictures around while delivering complicated lines, drawing, writing, and so on.

This sense of mobility within a static frame and the emphasis on a Brechtian distancing effect is what fascinates me the most in the complex relationship between the cinematic and the theatrical. I am not talking about the theatricality of performance as spectacle, but about the awareness that a performance which involves a distancing effect also foregrounds an ethics of representation: we all know that this is a performance and identification should not be at stake. What should be at stake instead is the space that I've preserved for you, viewers, a space for the expression of the critical function of subjectivity and free speech. This distancing effect is also at stake in the process of embodiment itself: the narrators are and are not the writers and activists portrayed. They literally embody multiple and complex identities. So while I was working on *The Tempest Society*, I thought of it as a play that could be performed for the camera alone, because the camera is the site where the 'performers' and the audience meet. The camera is the stage.

166

1
Jean-Luc Godard, *Histoire(s) du cinéma, Chapter 2: Seul le cinéma*, 1997. Godard suggests a definition of cinema as an art of resurrection. He subtly refers to *Orphée*, the film by Jean Cocteau that differs from the original Greek tale, as Eurydice is resurrected by 'death', performed by Maria Casarès. The film inspired many filmmakers, including Chris Marker, and Tarkovski.

2
Bouchra Khalili. Mixed media. Digital film, 15 photographs, 1 silkscreen print. 2015.

3
Jean Genet, *Preface to Soledad Brother: The Prison Letters of George Jackson*, 1970.

LE THEATRE ARABE DES TRAVAILLEURS IMMIGRES
PRESENTE:

"CA TRAVAILLE, CA TRAVAILLE
             ET CA FERME SA GUEULE"

Pièce écrite, montée et jouée par des travailleurs immigrés sur leurs
conditions de vie et de lutte, leurs conditions d'arrivée en France, les
difficultés quotidiennes, le racisme.
A l'occasion de la projection du film d'Heiny SROUR:
    "L'HEURE DE LA LIBERATION A SONNE" au cinéma 14 JUILLET
4, Bd Beaumarchais - Paris 11° -

SAMEDI 9 novembre 20 H et 22 H - SAMEDI 16 20h - 22h

"التمثيل العربي" للعمال المهاجرين

يقدم التمثيلية :

☆ اخدم اخدم أوسكرقمك ☆

كتبها عمال عرب وتعالج مشاكل حياتهم اليومية والعنصرية
مع الفيلم العربي على الثورة العربية في الخليج العربي للاخت
هني سرور

يوم السبت 9 و 16 نونبر
الساعة الثامنة والعاشرة مساءً

في قاعة السنماء "14 جويلي" 4 شارع بومارشي مترو باستيي
ناطق بالعربية والفرنسية

ΜΟΥΣΙΚΟ
ΙΝΤΕΡΛΟΥΔΙΟ

Musical Interlude

I'm a little refugee,
Ah, I tell you

My name is Malek

but I remain a Syrian
wherever I go

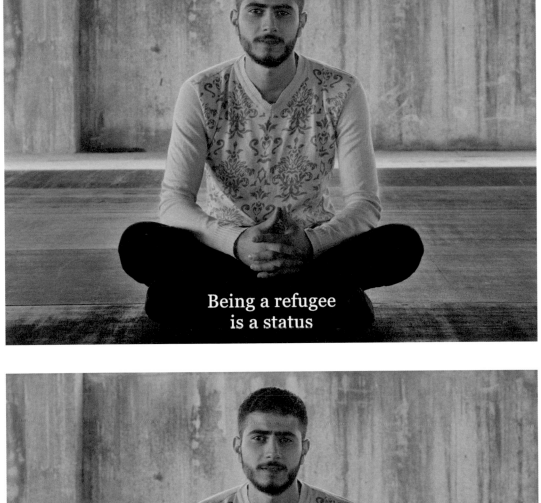

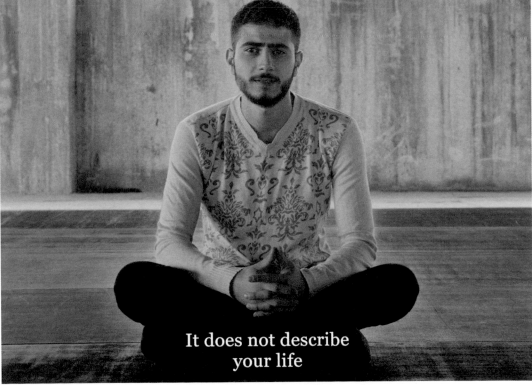

ici radio **assifa**

« La Tempête » — symbole de la volonté de l'immigration arabe de prendre la parole ; de combattre, au-delà des problèmes de chaque jour et du racisme, l'écrasement culturel auquel elle est soumise.

Cela fait des années que les immigrés arabes démontrent que — s'ils le sont aussi — ils ne sont pas seulement des ouvriers de chantier ou d'usine qui travaillent, travaillent, travaillent ; « ils savent aussi ouvrir leur gueule »... pour imposer leurs droits, l'existence de leur culture.

UNE RADIO IMMIGREE

La cassette « Radio ASSIFA » en sera la preuve. Chaque mois, elle rendra compte de la vie et des luttes qui écrivent peu à peu l'histoire de l'immigration arabe de France ; elle se fera l'écho de toutes les tentatives qui jettent les bases d'une nouvelle culture.

CHANSONS, INFORMATIONS...

Chaque cassette sera composée d'éléments entièrement originaux, qu'il s'agisse de la musique, des sketches de théâtre, des chansons, des témoignages ou des informations. Chaque cassette traitera aussi des problèmes surgis de l'actualité, donnera des nouvelles du pays et des conseils pratiques. Informations, chansons, poèmes, humour, une variété qui permettra de réécouter souvent et pendant longtemps ces cassettes.

PRENDRE LA PAROLE

« Radio ASSIFA » est réalisée par des Immigrés (membres de la troupe de théâtre Al Assifa, de groupes musicaux, militants du MTA, etc.) et par des Français, journalistes ou militants anti-racistes. « Radio ASSIFA » laissera aussi un maximum de place à ses auditeurs, à chacun de vous : n'hésitez pas à nous écrire, à nous envoyer vos idées, à nous proposer des poèmes, des chansons, des témoignages, des récits de votre vie en France, de ce qu'ont été les mouvements ou les guerres pour l'indépendance, des informations sur la situation au pays...

هنا
عاصفة
إذاعة العمال العرب
في فرنسا

ici radio **assifa**

| 1 Heure |

- Musique
- Informations
- Chansons
- Poèmes

ECRIVEZ-NOUS — FAITES CONNAITRE LA CASSETTE AUTOUR DE VOUS — ABONNEZ-VOUS —

Si vous ne trouvez pas la cassette :

ECRIVEZ-NOUS
P. FILLIOUD
B.P. 8 — 75521 — PARIS CEDEX 11

Chèques bancaires ou postaux à l'ordre d'IM. MEDIA.

Chaque cassette : 25 F (port compris)

ABONNEZ-VOUS
50 F POUR 3 CAS-SETTES (3 MOIS) — (+ 10 F POUR L'EX-PÉDITION) : SOIT 60 F A L'ORDRE D'IM. MEDIA

Édité par IM.MEDIA
imp.Spé.

based on
our stories:

how we left,
our whole journey from Syria,

Theatre is a space
for peace

Theatre respects
our words

That was a good enough reason
to engage with theatre

يوم ثقافي عربي

مقدم من طرف الأطفال والشباب العرب

في سبيل احياء ثقافتنا العربية

حفلة الأطفال يوم السبت 17 أفريل على 2 بعد الظهر

8 شارع   St Bruno   قاعة   Pierre L'ermite
باريس 18e   ميترو : لا ستابيل   n° la chapelle

journee CULTURELLE
ARABE

Animée par des jeunes et des enfants.

* Sketches — musique — chansons Arabes.

* Dessin présentés par les jeunes du quartier Barbès les enfants du 20°, de Nanterre, de Gennevilliers

* Theatre d'El-ASSIFA

samedi 17 avril 14h

8 bis rue Pierre l'ermite - Salle St Bruno
PARIS 18° metro la chapelle

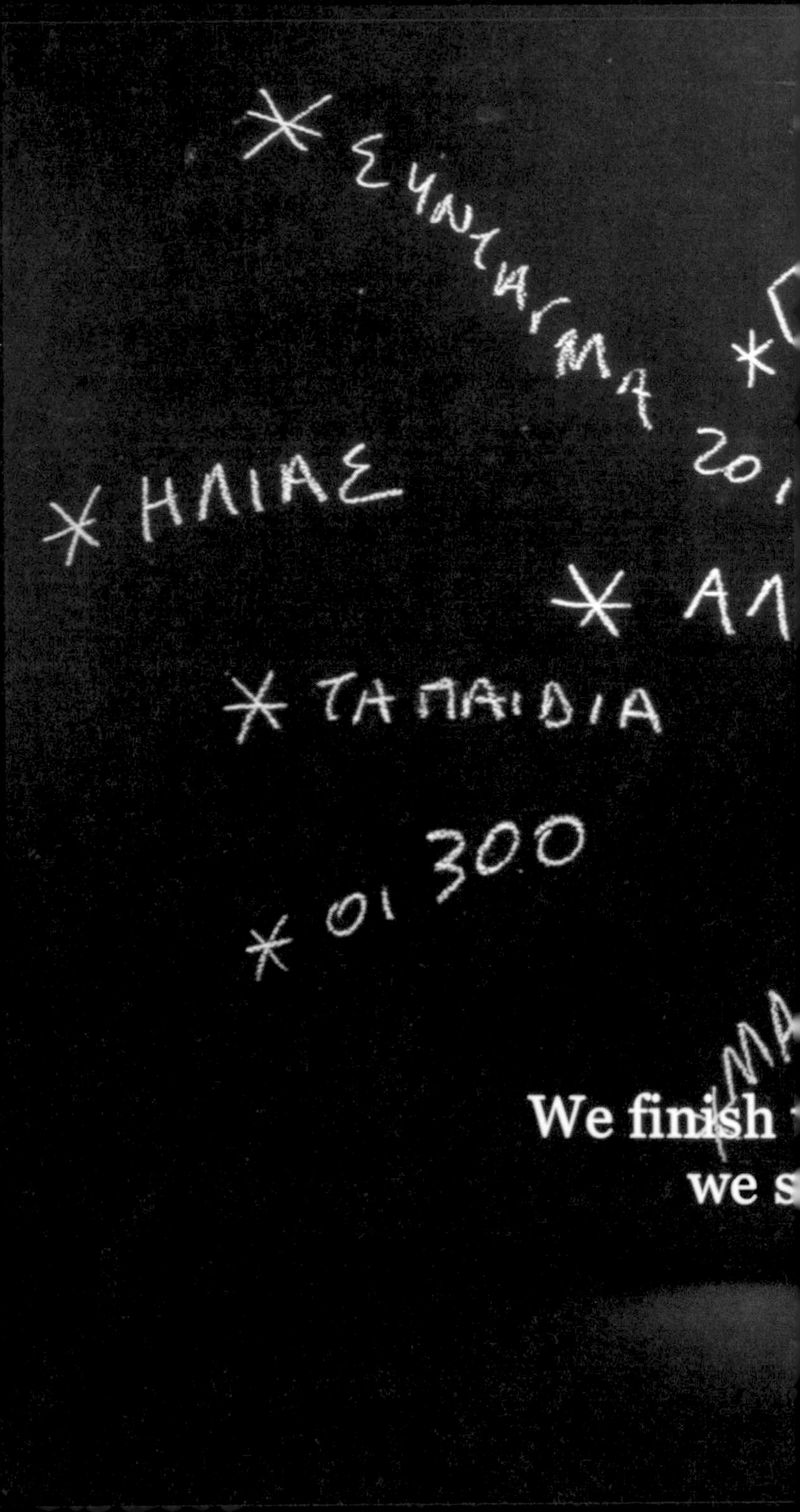

ΣΥΝΑΙΣΜΑ

20,

✳ ΗΛΙΑΣ

✳ ΑΛ

✳ ΤΑ ΠΑΙΔΙΑ

✳ ΟΙ 300

ΜΑ

We finish

we s

ZMENT

*ΓΑΝI

*KATEPINA

ΤΕΣΙΦΑ

*ΣΥΝΤΑΓΜΑ
2015

same way
ted,

ΣΥΝΤΑΓΜΑ
2015

Image Index

The Tempest Society, digital film, 60 mins, 2017.
Video stills, courtesy of the artist:

pp. 8–10, pp. 12–13, pp. 17–19, pp. 24–26, pp. 29–36,
p. 38, pp. 44–50, pp. 56–57, p. 89, pp. 94–95, pp. 108–113,
pp. 116–119, pp. 124–125, pp. 136–137, pp. 140–144,
pp. 148–149, pp. 152–159, pp. 169–171, pp. 174–179,
pp. 181–183, pp. 186–187, pp. 193–195.

Jacket: *The Tempest Society*, film poster collage, 2018

View of the installation at documenta 14, ASFA,
Athens, 2017. Photo by Stathis Mamalakis.
Courtesy Stathis Mamalakis:

pp. 42–43, pp. 76–77, pp. 90–91, pp. 106–107, pp. 114–115,
pp. 138–139, pp. 150–151, pp. 172–173, pp. 184–185,
pp. 190–191.

Al Assifa's performances, Collection Philippe Tancelin:

p. 11: Al Assifa, *Ça travaille, ça travaille, et ça ferme sa gueule*,
performance at Vincennes, Le Bassin, 1976.

p. 11: Al Assifa, parade, Halle de la Villette, 1974.

p. 20: Al Assifa performance at La Vie de Château, Paris, 1976.

p. 21: Al Assifa, *Ça travaille, ça travaille, et ça ferme sa
gueule*, Théâtre du Chêne Noir, Avignon, 1975.

pp. 22–23: Al Assifa, *Ça travaille, ça travaille, et ça ferme
sa gueule*, performance Paris, 1973.

p. 39: Philippe Tancelin, 1975.

p. 39: Al Assifa, *Ça travaille, ça travaille, et ça ferme
sa gueule*, Paris, 1973.

p. 51: 'Mokhtar' Bachiri at a parade in Barbès, Paris,
18th district. This image served as cover for the publication
of *Les Tiers Idées* in 1978.

p. 51: Parade in Barbès by Groupe Salve, a brother group
of Al Assifa, Mokhtar Bachiri (front), Philippe Tancelin
(back), 1978.

p. 52: Parade in Barbès, Geneviève Clancy, 1974.

p. 53: Al Assifa, *Ça travaille, ça travaille, et ça ferme
sa gueule*, 1974.

Images courtesy of Mogniss H. Abdallah.
© agence IM'média:

p. 37: Poster of the Call of Fatna Diab, sister of Mohamed
Diab, killed by a French policeman in the Versailles police
station, 1972. Committee for the Defence of the Life
and the Rights of Immigrant Workers. Original dimensions:
600 × 835mm.

p. 50: Performance of Al Assifa, Rennes, Britanny, February 12,
1977. 'At the invitation of immigrants support commitees,
Al Assifa performs a play on the working and living conditions
of immigrant workers in France'.

Al Assifa ephemera, collection Génériques/Odysséo:

pp. 54–55: 'At the invitation of the Diab committee and
the MTA (Movement of Arab Workers), Al Assifa performs
Ça travaille, ça travaille, et ça ferme sa gueule at the
Centre 8, in Versailles, in the outskirts of Paris'.

pp. 68–69: 'Al Assifa Collective, Theatre, Music, Poetry,
Radio, Information, Documentation. Members of the
collective: Groupe Salve (G. Clancy, P. Tancelin), Mokhtar
& Habib, Les Lézards, Bendir Déchaîné, Radio Assifa.'

pp. 92–93: 'Cultural gathering of Arab Workers. With Al Halaka
theatre group, and Arab Women Workers from Marseilles,
performing a play on the working conditions of Arab cleaning
ladies. With an Arab Folk Group made of Arab workers
from Clermont-Ferrand ; Moroccan workers from the
Chausson and General Motors factories ; and members
of the MTA (Movement of Arab Workers) from Paris, Aix,
Marseille, Toulon.'

p. 121: Poster of Al Assifa, 'Al Assifa performs, *Ça travaille,
ça travaille, et ça ferme sa gueule*'. On the right-hand
side of the poster are two drawings of a fedayeen. Al Assifa
named itself after the armed wing of Al Fatah.

pp. 122–123: El Halaka, brother group of Al Assifa. El Halaka
introduces its play *Vive La France, les Immigrés, Silence*
(Long Live France, Immigrants, Silence)'. El Halaka was
made up of seven members. 'Our play responds to the need
for struggle and change, and for the recovery of our culture.'

p. 145: 'A Call from Arab Workers to Belgian and Immigrant
Workers in Belgium. Arab Workers in France present a theatre
play on their working and living conditions, *Ça travaille,
ça travaille, et ça ferme sa gueule*. After touring in France,
their play will finally be performed in Belgium. All workers
and intellectuals are welcome to attend.'

p. 146: People's Festival organised by Al Assifa on the
occasion of May Day. 8.30pm. Salle Saint-Bruno, 8 rue
Pierre L'Hermite. Metro Barbès. Paris.

pp. 146–147: 'You're all welcome to the performance of
Ça travaille, ça travaille, et ça ferme sa gueule. A play
performed by Immigrant Workers. Free Entrance.'

pp. 160–161: Poster of La Vie de Château, a play by Al Assifa.
'Performance every Saturday at 8.30pm and Sunday at 4pm.
Salle Saint-Bruno, 8 rue Pierre L'Hermite. Metro Barbès, Paris.'

'Millions of men far from their land, our voice is made
of the voices of brothers remaining there, and of our
exile. Self-expression on a stage is ours, similar to the
streets where we demonstrate. We won't stop doing
both with the help and solidarity of the ones who always
supported us.
In the yard, the company, the university, where comrades
members of Al Assifa work, we take the stage together
in Barbès. These are the gestures and the voices that our
lives are made of.
Assifa for our rights. Assifa for our cultures. Assifa for
our humanity on all fronts.'

p. 167: 'The Arab Theatre of Immigrant Workers presents:
Ça travaille, ça travaille, et ça ferme sa gueule, a play
written, staged, and performed by immigrant workers on
their working and living conditions, their struggles, and
their arrival in France. On the occasion of the screening
of *The Hour of Liberation has come* by Heiny Srour.'

p. 169: Video still. The Tempest Society.

p. 180: Poster of Radio Assifa. 'A radio programme for
immigrant workers recorded on audio tape. Every month
Radio Assifa will give news of the struggles that are shaping

Film Credits

the History of Arab immigration in France. The tape will include original material: music, theatre, comedy sketches, information. Radio Assifa is produced by Immigrants, members of Al Assifa, music bands, and the MTA, along with French people, journalists, and anti-racist activists.'

pp. 188–189: Poster of an Arab Culture Day, jointly run by youth and children. 'Comedy sketches, music, and arabic songs. Exhibition of drawings by youth from Barbès, and children from Paris 20th district, Nanterre, and Gennevilliers. Performance by Al Assifa.'

Chers Camarades:

pp. 70–73: Video stills from *Chers Camarades* by Gérard Vidal, documentary, 93 mins, 2004. The stills originates from a short super 8 film captured by Vidal, then a worker at the Chausson factory in 1975. Al Assifa performed *Ça travaille, ça travaille, et ça ferme sa gueule* for the workers then on strike.

Drawing by Giannis Sotiriou:

pp. 131: Philippe's hand, courtesy of the artist, 2017.

The Tempest Society. Digital film. 2017. 60'.
Greek, French, Arabic, with English subtitles.
Commissioned for documenta 14.

Directed and Edited by Bouchra Khalili
Producers: Alexandre Kauffmann & Bouchra Khalili
Co-produced with Ibsen Awards
With the support of FNAGP, Paris
Additional support: Holland Festival (Amsterdam)
Special thanks for their support: Athens Festival,
Atopos cvc (Athens)

With by order of appearance:
Isavella Alopoudi
Elias Kiama Tzogonas
Giannis Sotiriou
Philippe Tancelin
Ghani
Katerina Barbojia
Malek Lazrae

With the participation of Gazmend Kapllani

Musical Interlude: *To prosfigaki* (c. 1930s), composition attributed to Nikos Sofroniou and Vangelis Papazaglou
Performed by: Angelos Angelo (voice and laouto),
Rémi Foucrier (violin), Kostas Tsarouchis (oud)

Interlude: The Children
Animation: Anna-Sofie Mathiasen
Drawings: Giannis Sotiriou

Cinematographer: Amine Berrada
Camera Assistants: Sotiris Konstas, Aigli Drakou
Sound Recording, Editing and Mixing:
Johannes Schmelzer-Ziringer
Sound Recording Assistant: Jan Moszumanski
Assistant Director: Nikoleta Leousl
Production Assistant: Erica Koukouna
Stage Technician: Maria Kakaroglou
Stage Technician: Akis Agrafiotis
Electrician: Ignatio Banilis
Video technician: Stratos Avramidis
Colorist: Gregor Pfüller
Research Assistant: Helle Siljeholm
Documentation: David Eisenschitz
Translation: Angeliki Poulou

Additional translations:
Isavella Alopoudi, Mazin Hussein, Bouchra Khalili,
Nikoleta Leousi, Giannis Sotiriou, Korinna Stathakou,
Elias Kiama Tzogonas, and Martin White.

The participants in this book include the collaborators in the film, Isavella Alopoudi, Elias Kiama Tzogonas, Giannis Sotiriou, along with Omar Berrada, Abdellali Hajjat, Pothiti Hantzaroula, Alexandre Kauffmann, Bouchra Khalili, and Philippe Tancelin, and translators Catherine Petit and Paul Buck. The work and legacy of the members of Al Assifa, and Pier Paolo Pasolini informs the contributions.

Contributors

ISAVELLA ALOPOUDI
was born in Thessaloniki. She lives and works in Athens. She was trained as a film producer and graduated from the Film Studies Department of Aristotle University of Thessaloniki, Faculty of Fine Arts. After spending a few years working for TV, she went back to her original vocation: cinema. She is currently working as an assistant producer at Neda Film, an Athens-based company, producing documentary films.

OMAR BERRADA
is a writer and curator, and the director of Dar al-Ma'mûn, a library and artists residency in Marrakech. He recently edited *The Africans* (2016), a book on migration and racial politics in Morocco, and curated exhibitions centering on the work and archive of writer and filmmaker Ahmed Bouanani. Omar was the guest curator of the 2017 Abraaj Group Art Prize and the 2018 *Forum 1:54* in Marrakech and New York, as well as a co-editor of Sharjah Biennial's web journal *tamawuj.org*. Currently living in New York, he teaches at The Cooper Union where he co-organises the IDS Lecture Series.

HENDRIK FOLKERTS
was recently appointed Dittmer Curator of Modern and Contemporary Art, at the Art Institute of Chicago. He previously held positions of global scope and impact as a curator at documenta 14, Kassel/Athens (2014–2018); as curator of performance, film & discursive programmes at the Stedelijk Museum, Amsterdam (2010–2015); and as the coordinator of the curatorial programme at De Appel arts centre, Amsterdam (2009–2011). Folkerts holds an MA in art history from the University of Amsterdam.

ABDELLALI HAJJAT
is Associate Professor of Political Science at the University of Paris Nanterre. His research focuses on the articulation of citizenship and race in French colonial and postcolonial law and urban uprisings and political mobilisations by postcolonial immigrants in working-class neighbourhoods, particularly in May '68 and afterwards. His published work includes, *Les Frontières de l'identité nationale*, (2012), *Islamophobia* with Marwan Mohammed, (2016), *Histoire politique des immigrations (post)coloniales. France 1920–2005* with Ahmed Boubeker (2008); and authored *The March for Equality and Against Racism* (2019). He is the principal coordinator of the *Dictionnaire biographique des mouvements immigrés en France*.

POTHITI HANTZAROULA
is Assistant Professor of Historical Anthropology in the Department of Social Anthropology and History at the University of the Aegean in Mytilene, Greece. She is a founding member of the Association of Oral History in Greece and one of the founding editors and member of the editorial board of the journal *Historein: A Review of the Past and Other Stories*. Her book *Sculpting subordination: Domestic workers in Greece at the first half of the twentieth century* (2012) is an oral history of paid domestic work in Greece. It was converted to a theatrical performance by the Group Casus Belli under the title 'On Subordination' (2013). Currently, she is working on a book on child survivors in Greece and their memory of the Shoah.

ALEXANDRE KAUFFMANN
graduated in literature and philosophy. He is an independent advisor for several film commissions focusing on supporting independent cinema from non-Western countries. He collaborates with Bouchra Khalili as a co-producer. Together, they have produced over twenty works in film and video that have been featured in exhibitions at MoMA (New York), Jeu de Paume (Paris), MACBA, (Barcelona), documenta 14 and the 55th Venice Biennale, as well as many other museums and international art exhibitions.

BOUCHRA KHALILI
is a Berlin-based Moroccan-French artist. Her work in film, installation, photography and printmaking has been shown in many international exhibitions including at documenta 14, the 55th Venice Biennale, the 18th Sydney Biennale, the 10th Sharjah Biennale. She has had solo exhibitions at MoMA (New York), PAMM (Miami), MACBA (Barcelona), Jeu de Paume (Paris), Secession (Vienna), among others. She was the recipient of several awards such as Ibsen Awards (2017), Abraaj Art Prize (2014), Sam Art Prize (2013–2015). In 2017–2018 she was a fellow at Harvard's Radcliffe Institute for Advanced Study. She is currently shortlisted for the Hugo Boss Prize 2018 and The Artes Mundi Prize 2018.

GIANNIS SOTIRIOU
was born in Athens, where he lives and works. He is a visual artist, working primarily with printmaking, drawing and scenography. He studied Fine Arts in Thessaloniki and is currently a student at the Athens School of Fine Arts, studying for his second degree. In 2017–2018, he also studied at Jan Matejko Academy of Fine Arts in Krakow through the Erasmus exchange student programme.

PHILIPPE TANCELIN
was born in Paris in 1948, and is a Professor Emeritus of Philosophy at Paris 8 University and a poet. His work in poetry focuses on the poetics of the transmission of history and the role of the witness. The author of thirty books, translated in fifteen languages, he is the editor in chief of the poetry series 'Poètes des cinq continents' (Poets of the five continents), published by L'Harmattan (Paris). A long-term activist committed to the support of oppressed minorities and colonised populations, Tancelin was a member of Al Assifa. In 1991, along with his sister Geneviève Clancy and Jean-Pierre Faye, he co-founded the CIPEP (Inter-University International Centre for the Creation of Poetical Spaces). In 2015, he founded the poetry collective 'EFFRACTION', gathering together fifty poets from all over the world. In January 2016, the collective published the book *Effraction 1: fragments et lambeaux*.

ELIAS KIAMA TZOGONAS
was born in Nairobi, Kenya. He moved to Athens at the age of 3. He graduated in April 2017 from the National and Kapodistrian University of Athens in pedagogy, psychology and philosophy studies. He is a member of Athens-based Afro-Greek artistic and educational activist groups. He teaches Greek language to refugees and migrants, and also supports applicants in preparing their interviews for naturalisation. Elias is also a painter of Byzantine icons.

The Tempest Society
Bouchra Khalili

Published by Book Works

Edited by Gavin Everall, and Lizzie Homersham
Translations by Catherine Petit & Paul Buck
Proofreading by Jenny Fisher
Designed by A Practice for Everyday Life
Typeset in Nobel Regular & Neuzeit S Book
Printed by Unicum, Netherlands
Printed on Lessebo Design and Profibulk 1.3
Distributed by Book Works

Book Works receives National Portfolio funding
from Arts Council England. This publication has
been generously supported by Galerie Polaris, Paris,
and ADN Galeria, Barcelona.

ISBN 978 1 906012 78 6

Book Works, 19 Holywell Row, London EC2A 4JB
www.bookworks.org.uk
Telephone: +44 (0)207 247 2203

Book Works would like to thank Bouchra Khalili and all the
contributors to this book, Phillipe Tancelin for permission
to translate extracts from *Les Tiers-Idées* by Geneviève
Clancy & Philippe Tancelin, Catherine Petit and Paul Buck
for translations from French to English of these extracts,
and of the essay by Abdellali Hajjat, and recognise the
generosity of the loan archives, photographer Stathis
Mamalakis, the funders of this book, ADN Galeria and
Galerie Polaris and our support from Arts Council England.

Bouchra Khalili would like to dedicate this book to the
memory of Mokhtar Bachiri, Saïd Bouziri, and Geneviève
Clancy. She expresses her deepest gratitude for their
support and contribution to:

A Practice for Everyday Life
agence IM'média
Mogniss H. Abdallah
Isavella Alopoudi
Katerina Barbojia
Omar Berrada
Hilde Guri Bohlin
Michelangelo Corsaro
Dalila Ennadre
David Eisenschitz
Gavin Everall
Marina Fokidis
Hendrik Folkerts
Collection Génériques / Odysséo
Ghani
Nacira Guénif-Souilamas
Abdellali Hajjat
Tifenn Hamonic
Pothiti Hantzaroula
Kai Johnsen
Maria Kallimani
Gazmend Kapllani
Alexandre Kauffmann
Malek Lazrae
Stathis Mamalakis
Pharoah Marsan
Bonaventure Soh Bejeng Ndikung
Oliver Ottenschläger
Jeanette Pacher
Christoph Platz
Jane Rolo
Tatiana Sagatni
Miguel A. Sánchez and ADN, Barcelona
Helle Siljeholm
Giannis Sotiriou
Adam Szymczyk
Philippe Tancelin
Katerina Tselou
Elias Kiama Tzogonas
Kelly Tsipni-Kolaza
Bernard Utudjian and Polaris, Paris